THE LEADER'S JOURNEY

Transforming Your Leadership to Achieve the Extraordinary

by

DONNA LICHAW

FOREWORD BY *Amy Jiménez Márquez*

TWO WAVES
BOOKS

TWO WAVES BOOKS

NEW YORK, NY, USA

"This book is for even the most reticent of leaders, those of us who aren't sure, deep-down, if we can truly show up for our team. With *The Leader's Journey*, Lichaw is right there by our side, teaming up so we can feel connected to the leader we want to be and make a plan for getting there."

—Lara Hogan,
author of *Resilient Management*

"Donna Lichaw gives us a leader's guide to being true to ourselves and developing our superpowers, as well as leading us through uncertainty to impact."

—Shay Howe,
CMO, ActiveCampaign, co-founder, Lead Honestly

"Have you ever asked yourself 'Why should anyone be led by me?' Let your story answer that question for you. *The Leader's Journey* teaches you how."

—Eduardo Ortiz,
CEO and co-founder, Coforma

"Donna Lichaw busts the myth that there's one uniform set of leadership qualities. Her latest book, *The Leader's Journey*, provides a path for discovering your unique superpowers and how to harness them effectively."

—Alexis Lloyd,
Senior UX Director, Google

"Donna uses incredible storytelling to provide actionable steps you'll need to become a better leader. *The Leader's Journey* crams years of executive coaching into a fast and engaging read."

—Tom Alterman,
Head of Product, Revenue, and Monetization, Asana

"Finally a book that doesn't treat leadership styles as one-size-fits-all. *The Leader's Journey* helped me think through how to tell my own story as a leader and use the superpowers I identified to lead more effectively. It will help you do the same!"

—Melissa Perri,
author of *Escaping the Build Trap* and
Senior Lecturer, Harvard Business School

"Donna's new book is a beautiful blueprint for finding clarity in the chaos of leadership and writing your own super story."

—Emily Davis,
Chief Product Officer, Skillcrush

"Lichaw brilliantly weaves together stories from her executive coaching practice and pop culture to deliver this secret decoder ring for discovering and understanding your superpowers, and how to use them to shape your story together with the heroes you lead."

—Scott Trudeau,
CTO, Listings Project

"Lichaw's book is easy-to-read, relatable, and gives advice that one can actually act on. It's a great read for those of us who are looking for some guidance and structure when it comes to professional growth."

—Fatima Husain,
Managing Director and General Partner, Mastry Ventures

The Leader's Journey
Transforming Your Leadership to Achieve the Extraordinary
By Donna Lichaw

Rosenfeld Media
125 Maiden Lane
New York, NY 10038
USA

On the Web: www.rosenfeldmedia.com
Please send errata to: errata@rosenfeldmedia.com

Publisher: Louis Rosenfeld
Managing Editor: Marta Justak
Interior Layout: Danielle Foster
Cover Design: Heads of State
Illustrator: MJ Broadbent
Indexer: Marilyn Augst
Proofreader: Sue Boshers

Contents at a Glance

Contents and Executive Summary

How to be the hero of your story as a leader and bring everyone along on your journey. Introducing a four-part framework
that makes superheroes—and leaders by extension—powerful
through identity, mission, superpowers, and impact.

Your core story of who you are as a leader can propel you forward—
or hold you back. Leverage your story to work for you, rather than
against you.

How your core identity narrative functions so that you can own
your story as a leader, rather than having it own you.

Shows you how to find your core identity narrative and
unlock your true story of who you are, where you're going,
why, and how.

Part II. Superpowers   33

How leadership superpowers work and how you can use them for good.

Chapter 3. Activate Your Superpowers   35

Uncover and activate your leadership superpowers.

Chapter 4. Manage Your Kryptonite   47

Find, accept, embrace, and ultimately leverage what holds you back, in order to move forward.

Part III. Mission   61

Map your mission as a leader and find the right path toward achieving your goals and making an impact.

Chapter 5. Backcast Your Future   63

Develop a strategic roadmap for what you want to accomplish in the world by thinking like a storyteller and starting with an incredible ending.

Chapter 6. Choose Your Own Adventure   89

Prototype, troubleshoot, and keep moving forward when you face tough decisions, cliffs, and forks in the road along your journey.

Chapter 7. Tame Your Horror Stories   97

Leverage your deepest, darkest fears and transform them from impediments to strategic assets.

Part IV. Impact   117

Leaders never work alone. Learn how to make the impact you want to make—on others and the world.

Foreword

As someone who once thought she had a meandering path into leadership, I have been looking forward to this book since I learned it was being written by Donna Lichaw. Like many of my colleagues in the profession of user experience design, I started out rather organically. I graduated with degrees in Theater Arts. I figured I could do one of two things: try my luck in the entertainment industry or teach theater. To Hollywood I went. I worked at a special effects company in North Hollywood as my day job, creating print brochures and doing other odd tasks. The Creative Director said "Hey, can you look into this web thing? I think we're gonna need one of those websites." And that was the beginning of my journey.

How I got from a grunt at a special effects company to VP of Design at a tech company was something I thought was circuitous, until I realized that my values, the stories I told myself, and my superpowers were what led me there. I came to understand that I thrive on ambiguity and learning, and am mission-driven to work in an environment where I can make people's lives better and more joyful. Understanding that helps me see my future path more clearly and circumvent false narratives in my own mind about the value I bring as a design leader and my ability to execute my work effectively.

Understanding how you got where you are helps you get where you need to go. If you aren't sure where your career as a leader is…well… leading, are fearful of where it's heading, or just plain feel stuck, Donna Lichaw is the right person to help.

In *The Leader's Journey*, Donna shares the tools she's gleaned from her background in storytelling and filmmaking, and has used for her clients in her extensive executive coaching career. She provides compelling examples of how these tools have been helpful with her clients so that you can build your own understanding of your superpowers, your super foibles (aka kryptonite), your "why," and define—and plot—a leader's journey for success in your future.

—Amy Jiménez Márquez
Design leader, speaker, mentor

We Can Be Heroes

When my niece turned three, my partner, Erica, and I bought her a superhero dress for her birthday. It had bright colors and a removeable cape. It was awesome. As soon as she unwrapped her gift, my niece immediately changed into her new dress, struck a superhero pose with her arms flexed up into the air, and proclaimed, "I'm a superhero!"

We assumed she would wear this dress a few times, outgrow it, and that would be that. What we didn't expect was that she would wear this dress as much as possible for the next three years, even after outgrowing it. The more she wore it, the more super she felt and the more super she acted. She eventually passed it on to her little sister who used it in much the same way.

When you're three years old, being a superhero is as easy as putting on a costume and proclaiming as much. We even have a name for it—the *Batman Effect*. Studies show that when children put on a costume, they are more confident and resilient.[1] For the rest of us, it's not that simple. But it can be easily learned. And it's oh so important. I learned this the hard way.

A few years ago, I was asked to facilitate a business storytelling workshop during an offsite leadership retreat for one of the most successful tech companies on the planet. I had just published my book, *The User's Journey*, which was all about helping people engage their users by building products and services with a compelling, foundational story of how their customers thought about, used, and found value in their products. Customers need to be the hero, I argued. They have important things they need to do with the products they buy—they need to slay some dragons. And the job of someone who builds tech products is to help them do that.

Before I arrived at the offsite meeting, I asked a bunch of the leaders who would be in attendance what they thought would make the workshop successful. As I listened to their responses, I had an inkling that something was wrong because it seemed to me that each of these leaders was experiencing *people* problems, not *product* problems.

But there was just one other thing: The workshop I was under contract to deliver was focused on *software* and *apps*, not people As such, it was meant to help these executives understand, design for, and communicate customer problems so they could better align their teams toward a collective vision, inspire them, and move them to action. But it wouldn't help them resolve internal people conflicts that had nothing to do with customers or software. Immediately, and with great reluctance, I realized that the workshop I was planning to deliver was *not* the right workshop for this team.

1. Rachel White, Emily Prager, Catherine Schaefer, Ethan Kross, Angela Duckworth, and Stephanie Carlson, "The 'Batman Effect': Improving Perseverance in Young Children," *Child Development* 88, no. 5 (2017): 1563–1571, https://doi.org/10.1111/cdev.12695.

I didn't want to waste anyone's time, so I told my client that my workshop was geared toward successful product leadership, but the real problem for them was that there were a lot of interpersonal conflicts among teams. Frankly, that was something I wasn't prepared to help with.

"No, no, no—it's fine" was their response. "Every team has similar problems. We're working on it. But in the meantime, they need to get better at storytelling. They need to get better at influencing other people and convincing them to do things. They don't know how to do that."

Reassured by my client, I agreed to proceed with the workshop I had planned. I heard this from a lot of businesses at the time and still hear it today: people think that telling stories is some kind of a panacea that will help leaders be more effective. I wanted to believe this, so I convinced myself that it was true. I would eventually learn that this was a tiny piece of a much bigger story about what makes leaders great.

Months later, I finally arrived in Napa Valley to conduct the workshop. I was excited to work with this team and help them become more effective. So when we finished the morning session, I felt pretty good about it and hoped I was at the top of my game. These amazing executives were fully engaged in the workshop, and I was certain I was delivering tremendous value to them, and by extension, to this remarkably successful tech business.

That is, until, one by one, a few of the executives in attendance came up to me during lunch and gave me much the same blunt feedback (being blunt is one of the superpowers the people at this tech goliath possess): "This is cool, and I got some great info out of the session, but I don't see how it's going to help me with my real problem."

I felt embarrassed and ashamed, and I knew deep in my gut that something felt off, although at this point I didn't really know how to trust my gut instincts. I asked these executives who brought me their blunt (but spot-on) feedback to explain exactly where I had missed the mark, and they told me.

"Aligning people toward a product vision is not our biggest problem," one of the workshop participants said. "Our products are successful. Our company is successful. My problem is this: How do I get people not just to listen to the stories I tell them, but to actually listen to me, to connect with me, to work with me?"

I asked him to tell me what was really going on.

"OK, here's the scoop. My head of engineering hates me. Her engineers don't listen to my product managers. My product managers don't listen to me half the time. Our head of marketing is so checked out that he bypasses us entirely, even though they're supposed to loop us in early. Our products get built but my team is frustrated. The teams we work with are frustrated. I'm frustrated. My performance evaluations suffer. Attrition is becoming a problem. We're starting to miss deadlines. I feel bad about all this, and I don't know what to do."

"Wow," I replied. "That's a lot."

"Can't I be a hero?" he asked me. "Our customers are fine. They're not going anywhere. How can I be a hero?"

I thought about it for a minute and responded, almost reflexively, "This is not about you. You need to turn everyone you work with into heroes. That's how you're going to be a hero. You start with the customer. Then you focus on your business, your organization, your team—align them, excite them, enlist them—and then you make it all happen. We'll cover most of that this afternoon."

As soon as these words came out of my mouth, I realized how wrong this all sounded. I had seen this work time and time again—for my clients, for me as a consultant, and when I worked in-house as a product leader. And this is how a lot of folks in the tech world viewed successful technical leadership. Customer first. User-centered. This is how we operated. It was literally written into this company's employee handbook. But it suddenly felt like I was missing something.

"Hmmm—I don't think that's it," he said before walking away.

In the 1980 film, *Superman II*, there's a scene where Lois Lane falls off the side of a building. As she's falling, Superman swoops in to save her. "I've got you," he confidently says as they float in mid-air high above Metropolis. "You've got me? Who's got you?!" she asks, dumbfounded. That day in Napa, I wanted to be Superman swooping in to help the team. But I didn't feel like much of a hero. I was missing my cape. More importantly, this executive was missing his cape. And products were not the answer.

At the end of the day, I left the offsite feeling like I had failed, but spurred on to figure out what the correct answer was. I knew there was a way for this executive to feel like a hero. I'd seen it happen before, and I'd personally experienced it as an in-house leader, speaker, author, and business owner. And he was right—telling stories about customers or being unified in what you were building with your team was *not* enough. But other than telling this leader, "I don't know, you should go work with an executive coach or talk to your therapist," I didn't have the answer. Not yet. Frankly, this was the most important workshop of my career, and I really wanted to please these people. But I had to spend a few years learning how to do much of what all of the characters in the book go through to learn how to do that—to trust my gut and write my own story, rather than have others write it for me.

How Superheroes Work

Five years, thousands of hours of research and practice with some of the most amazing leaders on the planet, and an entire business pivot later, here's what I learned and will teach you how to do in this book: If you want to be a great leader, you can't just be a hero. You have to be a superhero.

Leadership is hard! It's a pressure cooker of needing to self-actualize and take care of others. You need to do things you never imagined you could do. One minute you might need to leap over buildings in a single bound. The next you need to rescue a kitten from a tree. It all requires strength, speed, and agility. And yes, it sometimes even requires a cape.

Superheroes—and the superhero genre by extension—have some key identifying characteristics. Every superhero has a set of superpowers, a mission, and a unique identity that often signifies or personifies those superpowers, mission, or both. These characteristics are inseparably intertwined.[2] Through finding out who they are, using their superpowers for good, and accomplishing their mission, superheroes save the day. They are powerful and make their biggest impact when they get this cocktail right.

---

2. Robin S. Rosenberg and Peter Coogan, eds., *What Is a Superhero?* (New York: Oxford University Press, 2013).

But being a superhero isn't easy. Superheroes manage lots of conflict—internal and external. They battle supervillains. They battle themselves. They need to engage themselves constantly and everyone around them as they lose and gain superpowers, lose sight of and regain sight of their mission, and find and refine their identity.

Superheroes never work alone. Even Batman, who has a propensity toward operating as a loner, has a sidekick (Robin), an assistant (Alfred), and is a founding member of The Justice League—a team of superheroes.

Superheroes not only have a story. Superheroes *are* the story. Spider-Man, for example, is not just the hero of an adventure tale. Spider-Man is the story of a boy who learns to embrace his identity, superpowers, and mission.

Leadership is much the same. You have to know who you are, activate your superpowers, map your mission, and engage yourself, others, and the world so that you can get where you want to go and make the impact you want to make.

When you think of superheroes, you might imagine them as (mostly) white (mostly) men who are in the natural position to accomplish anything they want in the world. Think it, be it, and go make it. That's not realistic for a lot of us. While being a great leader shares a lot with being a superhero, this does not mean that you have to be a privileged, straight white dude in order to do this. Being a superhero isn't just about self-fulfillment and accomplishment. It's about embracing otherness, embracing others, embracing differences, and embracing yourself. Superheroes are by nature aliens. They're freaks. They're mutants from other planets. They don't quite belong.

That's part of the beauty of superheroes, why so many people identify with them, and why they're an apt metaphor for leaders in an ever-changing, diverse world. For example, Superman was a humanoid, English-speaking alien (from the planet Krypton) without a home (his planet had exploded). He learned how to blend in with the Americans he lived and worked with, but he never really belonged. And he had superpowers that he had to figure out how to use toward good during the course of his life journey. Superhero stories are about finding differences, understanding how those differences impact the world, and then using them for good.

I have worked with hundreds of successful leaders all around the world. The people who come to me the most and bashfully proclaim, "Hey, I'm a superhero. Can I work with you?" are often women, queer folks, and underrepresented people who don't quite fit in. When you don't look and act like everyone else, showing up is unfortunately not enough. This is the case whether they are a CEO or a newly promoted manager.

Even many of my lovely, straight white dude clients—whether they own the company or work for someone else—feel like that strange weirdo who never quite learned how to fit in. It can feel lonely at the top. And by design, as a leader, you are not like everyone else you work with. When you can embrace your otherness and learn how to harness it to connect better with yourself and others, that's when the magic happens.

The Story Starts with You

When you figure out who you are as a leader, your story starts with you, ripples out to those you work with, and then it travels outside the walls of your organization—to your customers and the communities in which you do business. As you lead yourself, lead others, and lead your business, you bring that epic story to life.

So, how do you find your story? Fortunately, there's no right or wrong way to approach it. If you had asked comic book maven, Stan Lee, what approach he would take, he would have told you to start with the super-powers and then craft your story around that. Other people like to start stories at the end and work their way forward from the beginning. Yet others start with conflict, a problem, or a challenge.

While this book is not about writing or storytelling in any traditional sense, the most effective way to find your story as a leader is by think-ing and working like a storyteller. You break things apart. Then you put them back together again. And then you make them real.

This book is accordingly broken into four parts. In Part I: "Identity," you will take a step back and assess the big-picture vision of who you are, where you're going, what you've accomplished, how, why, and when. In Part II: "Superpowers," you will learn how to find and acti-vate your superpowers. In Part III: "Mission," you'll learn how to see the stories in every journey you take as a leader so that you can better align toward your mission and create the impact you want. In Part IV: "Impact," you will learn how to put it all together and apply what you've learned toward engaging yourself and everyone you work with so that you accomplish your goals and achieve the extraordinary.

While this book is linear, leading like a superhero is not. All leaders need an identity, superpowers, and a mission, but you don't need to find them in that order. They are as inextricably intertwined as a hero and her story. What is key, however, is that you have your center intact. That's where your power comes from.

Are you ready?

Let's go!

I

Identity

Find out who you are and do it on purpose.

—Dolly Parton

1

Your Core Identity Narrative

A superhero's identity is signified by their costume or a nickname. But it is much more than that. It's the story of who they are. For example, Superman's costume that is made of alien material, featuring a large "S," tells us about who he is (a superhuman alien) and what he can do (fly). Captain America's red, white, and blue star-spangled uniform and shield tell us about his beliefs and mission—he stands for freedom and shields the oppressed. Buffy the Vampire Slayer, on the other hand, doesn't wear a costume at all. Her name clearly signifies what she does: she slays vampires. A superhero's identity encapsulates her story of who she is, where she is going (mission), and how she will get there (superpowers).

But superheroes are often wrong about their identity early on in their journey. As such, they are not super yet. For example, before Harry Potter found out that he was a wizard destined to save the world, he was an orphan who lived under the stairs at his aunt and uncle's house. He was an outcast in his family with the uncanny ability to wreak havoc with his mysterious, as-yet unidentified powers. It's only when he found out his true identity that he could learn magic and then lead himself, lead others, and save the world.

When you find out who you are and how to leverage that, your story really gets going. I learned this the hard way.

When I left that leadership retreat in Napa that day I could not stop thinking about that executive's question. *How can I be a hero?* I wish I could say that my mission was clear, superpowers activated, and I confidently set out on my quest to find out how leaders could be heroes, transforming my business and myself, as a result. I transformed from someone who developed products to someone who developed people. I found my cape. I helped others find their capes. We all lived happily ever after. The end.

But leadership journeys are rarely that straightforward.

I eventually did those things. But first, I flew home feeling like a failure and spiraled into a debilitating depression. The worse I felt, the harder it was to muscle through some of the biggest projects of my career. I'm embarrassed to admit that I did not show up as my best self as I delivered keynote addresses and consulted with teams and companies that I was sure I was letting down. I wanted to put the brakes on my software development work and focus on my new obsession. But I refused to give in to my whims. I had a very good reason for doing that—I knew that deep down, I was a quitter. When I found success, I quit and moved onto something new. I wasn't going to let that happen again.

As I would eventually learn, this story wasn't totally true. But it felt true. As such, it had a strong power over me. Psychologists call this kind of story an *identity narrative*—the story of who you are. I didn't realize this at the time, but this story was also my cape—only at this point in my journey, it was choking me rather than helping me fly.

We all have stories that guide us. They move us forward. And they hold us back. It is only when you see them for what they are that you can embrace the ones that move you forward and transform the ones that hold you back.

To understand how to do this, you have to know what you're looking for. To know what you're looking for, you have to understand how stories work.

Stories Create Understanding

People have told stories since they began to communicate. The earliest evidence of storytelling, dates back 36,000 years.[1] It's believed that stories evolved as a way for people to teach one another so that they could influence behavior and ultimately stay alive.

For example, let's say that your clan lives not far from a river, and little Lucy wants to go down to the river alone to play. You might tell Lucy, "I told you before, don't go down to the river alone. It's dangerous." She might listen to you, or she might not. If you have ever dealt with a toddler or worked with an adult who behaves like a toddler, you know that they don't often want to listen. Our hardwired need for autonomy starts at a very young age.

Instead, you could tell Lucy a story: "Lucy, once upon a time, little Timmy went down to the river alone. He slipped in the mud along the bank, fell into a deep pool of water, and died a painful death while

---

1.   Joshua Hammer, "Finally, the Beauty of France's Chauvet Cave Makes Its Grand Public Debut," *Smithsonian* (April 2015), www.smithsonianmag.com/history/france-chauvet-cave-makes-grand-debut-180954582/

being chewed on by a crocodile. We could hear him screaming from the terrible pain he suffered as he was being torn apart. By the time we ran down to the river to help, it was too late. All we found was one of his shoes. So, whenever you go to the river, always take someone with you." That story is much more likely to stick with Lucy and to have your desired outcome.

At their best, your stories move you forward. They motivate, inspire, and move you to action. They keep you smart and safe. They keep you alive.

At their best, these stories also hold you back. They keep you safe from doing stupid things—like changing your business focus just when things are getting good.

Stories elicit feelings and feelings guide behavior.

But stories aren't just for telling. To process your story and then take action, Lucy needs to glean meaning from your story. Stories are how you comprehend what has happened, is happening, and will happen in the future if you take action. If things work out, you get to be the hero. Otherwise, you die.

Stories are the currency of understanding.

But it would be inefficient if you had to constantly hear people telling you stories in order to stay alive. Over time, the stories that you hear become a part of how you operate—you integrate them into your values, beliefs, sense of self, and projections onto the past, future, and even other people. They become so much a part of you that you don't realize they're there. Thinking in stories is like breathing or walking—you do it without noticing it. It's just how you operate.

Stories are an evolutionary feature. They're a huge part of how humans got this far.

But stories are also a bug—a defect, a glitch. When they go wrong, they go terribly wrong. To see what to do about it, I want to introduce you to Oscar.

Oscar was once a patient working with psychologist, Stephen Madigan, a pioneer in the field of narrative therapy. When Oscar first met Madigan, he was isolated, depressed, and suicidal. The previous year, he had been hit by a truck while crossing the street and immediately fell into a coma. He awoke after three months and endured a long, arduous recovery. He survived, surprising everyone including his doctors.

But he was debilitated by severe anxiety and no longer wanted to live. At the time that Oscar sought treatment with Madigan, he believed that he was a "good for nothing," a "useless human being."[2] While this story wasn't true, Oscar believed it to be true. It was powerful enough to compel him to want to end his life.

Stories started to be used as a serious therapeutic tool many decades ago. Typically, when you go into a clinical setting with a problem, you are diagnosed by a professional and receive a prescription. *You are depressed. Do this.* You are ascribed a story and prescribed an ending. The results of a traditional, diagnostic approach are hit or miss, however. After all, we humans don't always love being told what to do.

Starting in the 1980s, narrative psychologists and therapists like Madigan started to have a different idea. What if you let people take ownership of their stories rather than have doctors ascribe and prescribe a story to them? Might they have enough agency that they could then author their own way forward? The answer that Madigan found with Oscar was *yes*.[3]

When you restructure your narrative, you can change your behavior and change yourself.

Finding Your Narrative

When Madigan and Oscar unpacked his story, they saw that they didn't have a lot of data at its foundation. He felt unwell, he had a difficult recovery, he was convinced that his partner would abandon him, his friends would find him out, and he did not want to live. This all amounted to one epic story with a lot of missing pieces.

2. Stephen Madigan, *Narrative Therapy*. Theories of Psychotherapy Series, 2nd ed. (Washington D.C.: American Psychological Association, 2019).
3. Michael White, *Maps of Narrative Practice* (New York: WW Norton, 2007).

To fill in the missing pieces, Oscar and Madigan enlisted friends and family to write a brief letter expressing how they remembered him, how they currently felt about him, and how they imagined their relationship in the future. The letters poured in.

What Oscar thought was true was anything but true. He wasn't useless and unloved. He was missed and much-loved. These stories created a much more cohesive, truthful story. It didn't happen overnight. It took time, mindfulness, and having new experiences with his friends and family that could overwrite the former story. Over time Oscar transformed from an anxious, depressed "good for nothing" to a calm, confident friend and partner to many people. In transforming his story, he transformed himself. Oscar learned how to be the hero of his story.

When I first learned about Oscar and narrative therapy, I decided to take a closer look at my own story that was holding me back. This story was true, as far as I could tell. I was there! I lived it. I was living it. Could I really rewrite it?

Yes and no.

Although talking with people who shape your narrative and hearing their stories firsthand is the most effective way to reshape your story (more on that in Chapter 8, "Assessing Your Impact"), it's not always possible. My story started when I was eight years old. If I could have, I would have gone back to the source. But my mom passed away when I was 13 years old. This story was all I had.

So, I did the next best thing. I unpacked this story like a screenwriter would. I broke my story into little pieces to see if I was missing anything. And then I put it back together and made it more complete.

My story started one day when I wanted to learn how to play piano and begged my mom for lessons. But lessons were expensive. Pianos were even more expensive. And I had a tendency to pick up new hobbies and drop them. The answer was emphatically "*No*." I begged and begged, and the answer eventually became, "But you always start things and then you stop them. Lessons are expensive. Pianos are expensive. No."

I eventually got those piano lessons, and I loved them. Convinced that I would stick with this hobby, my parents saved up enough money to buy me a piano. Two years later, I got bored, asked to quit, and got a big "I told you so" from my mom. I cost my family a lot of money. My parents were upset. And I felt ashamed. I regretted not listening to my mom. She was right all along.

I carried this story—and this shame—with me like a suit of armor for the next 30 years. "Don't quit," I told myself whenever I got excited about something new. And quit, I would.

While this story had always felt cohesive to me, it was missing some key components.

Understanding Narrative Structure

At its core, every story has a beginning, a middle, and an end. And every story has a *protagonist*. That's the hero—sometimes a group of heroes.

Every hero wants to accomplish something—they are either intrinsically motivated, or they find out that they are called to do something. This is what is called a *call to adventure* or a *call to action*. For example, Batman doesn't fight villains for fun. He is called to do so after his parents are mugged and killed when he is a child. Buffy the Vampire Slayer is called to action by an ancient Watcher's Council.

Along their journey, every hero faces conflict—both inner and outer.

And, in the end, they resolve their conflict and meet their goals. If they don't, it's a cliff-hanger or a tragedy.

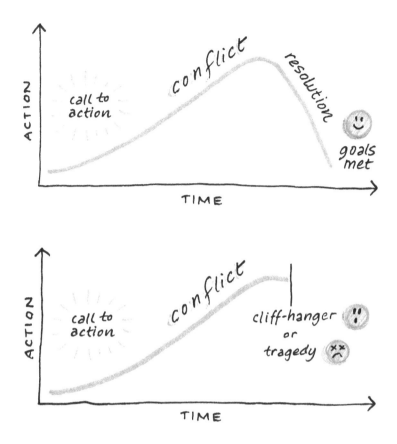

But for a story to be great, goals are not enough. A hero must have a reason for wanting to meet their goals. A *so that…* or *why*. These reasons often come down to basic human needs like food, shelter, love, connection, certainty, knowledge, mastery, autonomy, being understood, or being of service to name a few.[4] (For a comprehensive list of human needs, download a free Needs Decoder Ring from my Story Driven Leadership Toolkit: www.donnalichaw.com/toolkit.)

4. Daniel H. Pink, *Drive: The Surprising Truth About What Motivates Us* (New York: Riverhead Books, 2011) and Marshall B. Rosenberg, *Nonviolent Communication: A Language of Life: Life-Changing Tools for Healthy Relationships*, 3rd ed. (Encinitas, CA: PuddleDancer Press, 2015).

For example, Batman defeats villains to uphold justice. He could do it to seek vengeance (this is the case early on), but he would be a very different hero (an anti-hero) with a very different story. He could do it for no reason, but that would be boring. Heroes need a bigger purpose in life so that we can believe, relate, and connect to them.

While stories can get much more complex than this, this core architecture is what storytellers use to write stories. It's also what your brain uses to understand and experience stories.

When I broke apart my story like a storyteller, I realized that it was missing a key component: a proper ending. A *so that*…

In my story, my hero knew what she wanted, but she didn't understand deep down why she wanted it. I wanted to play piano. I played piano. Boring story. Boring ending. I wanted to play guitar. I played guitar. Same. "But *why*?" When I really thought about it, I wanted to express myself.

Simple reason. Totally different story.

As I got clear on the real ending of this story, I realized that I had actually accomplished what I had set out to do that day when I was eight years old. I just couldn't see it because I had the ending all wrong. I figured out how to express myself. I had an amazing time doing it. After learning to play many, many instruments that I liked, but didn't love, I eventually learned to play guitar. I found my thing. I spent the next few decades playing in rock bands. I met my best friends, met my mentors, kicked off my career in tech, and eventually met my wife through playing music.

Looking at my story with a proper ending, I could see for the first time in my life that this wasn't the story of a quitter. This was the story of someone who did not give up.

When I applied this story to my leadership journey, I realized that my story was much the same. What I always thought of as a series of failures, was in reality a decades-long career at the forefront of the tech industry. I wasn't a quitter. I was an expert and a leader in my field.

When I saw an opportunity, I pounced. I had grit—something a lot of leaders strive for. Not giving up until I found what I was looking for was a part of my process and my journey. I just couldn't see it before.

As I saw all of this, my anxiety started to lift, and I began to feel like a human again. Where I used to feel ashamed, I now wished my mom could see how my story had turned out—how I had turned out. She would have been so proud. I was proud. I am proud.

Once I could see my story—and therefore see myself—I quit developing software and started developing leaders. I found my courage. I found my cape. And the world is a better place for it. And because this is a business leadership book, I should also mention that my business is much more successful because of it. It wouldn't be easy—still isn't. But that's all part of the leader's journey.

I would have a lot of work to do to fully believe this new story and put my old one to rest. But it piqued my curiosity enough to see if I could apply what I learned toward helping leaders unlock their own stories. Because I am someone who does not give up, the answer is a resounding *yes*. Throughout this book, I will show you exactly how to do that.

2

Unlocking Your Story

When Lisa came to me for help, I had completely pivoted my software development business to leadership development. My sole focus was—and still is—to help leaders and teams transform their leadership so they could lead their businesses forward more effectively.

Lisa was trying to do this but felt stuck. She had just been promoted to the head of digital products and services for one of the most successful public radio stations in the country. It was a high-profile, prominent, and important job in an industry that was undergoing a huge transformation into digital products, services, and content. Lisa's boss, the CEO of the organization, was relatively new and had a mandate to transform and grow the organization to elevate its status as an industry leader. They had big hopes and dreams. But it was harder than they both expected.

"I'm too quiet," Lisa admitted to me when we first met. "I don't know if I can do this."

"Do what?" I asked.

"Be what my boss needs me to be."

"What do they want you to be?"

"Loud," she said. "I mean, I know I can do the technical part of my job, but the leadership stuff is so hard. I'm disappointing my boss, disappointing my team, disappointing myself."

When he first promoted Lisa, the CEO told her that he believed she could do the job, but she needed to act more like a leader. In particular, she needed to speak up more often. Over time, this feedback from Lisa's boss got louder and louder. And the louder the feedback got, the quieter Lisa became.

In meetings, and in her day-to-day interactions, Lisa had a hard time speaking up—she was naturally quiet and shy. It was becoming a real problem for her. Her boss brought in an executive coach to help her, but it only made things worse. The more her coach tried to tell her how to do her job, the quieter she became.

This was embarrassing for Lisa because she interacted with many key players in her job—executives, board members, donors, technical engineers—many of whom were quite loud and boisterous. One day she'd be in a meeting with a brash, seasoned media executive, the next day with the head of audio engineering who had been doing his job for 30 years and had no desire to change anything, and another day with donors, many of whom were public figures with strong opinions about what their money and reputation should be used to create.

As with many narratives, it was a story that she had carried deep inside her since childhood—at home, at school, and eventually at work. Since other people told her that story, too, she knew it was true.

As people wrote Lisa's story for her, she was in the back seat not enjoying the ride. She could let her story own her thoughts, emotions, and actions. Or she could find her true story—and amplify that.

Typically, when leaders come to me for help, they have a long laundry list of characteristics and skills they think they need to possess to lead effectively. Sometimes this comes from self-assessment—for example, they think they can't manage their time. Sometimes it comes from other people—they are told that they're a micromanager. And often it's a combination of both.

For every Lisa who is told she doesn't speak up enough, there is a Mirai who is told to be less domineering if she wants to be accepted by the boys' club. For every Toby who is told that they need to be more command-and-control, there is a Bogdan who is told that he needs to stop telling people what to do. When they're leveling up, rising quickly, or rapidly scaling, many leaders and teams want to be—or are told to be—something that they are not.

There are usually good reasons for people wanting to change themselves or those around them. Maybe they suddenly see increased attrition, disengagement, or unmet performance or business goals across their team. Or maybe things are going great, but management or their board doesn't trust their leadership because they don't fit the bill of what they think a leader should look like, act like, or be like. In tech, this happens a lot as more women and underrepresented leaders advance and as startups rapidly scale past their comfort level.

Other times, there are no problems, no external expectations, and it all comes from within. A lot of us internalize the predominant narrative of what a leader should be—opinionated, eloquent, decisive, domineering, and so on—and don't know how to live up to or even counter that effectively. We spend a lot of time worrying about stuff like this, and ultimately show up as half the leader we want to be or half the team we need to be. Why? Because our energy isn't spent on what it should be doing—leading.

But here's the thing: Trying to be someone you are not is a waste of time. When you're so attuned to what's going wrong, you can't see what's working well or have the energy to cultivate it. The flip side is also true. When you pause, step back, and look for what's working with your leadership, you will find out who you are. When you can be more of who you are, that's when the magic happens.

Just like Harry Potter, Buffy, Superman, or whoever your favorite superhero is, you have a story waiting to be told. You just need to know how to find it. Then you bring it to life by *being* it. This is what Lisa learned how to do.

Breaking Your Story

During my first meeting with Lisa, I felt an uncanny disconnect between who she said she was and how I experienced her to be. Because as she recounted her story to me of a quiet, insecure failure, she was anything but quiet. She spoke with clarity, confidence, and a lot of energy. The Lisa I saw in front of me seemed like a different person than the one she described. I asked if she noticed that.

"Yeah," she said. "I'm pretty determined to fix this. But I need to do it in a way that feels good to me. My last coach kept trying to tell me to do things his way, and it just didn't work."

"So, you speak up when you feel determined?" I asked.

"Huh," she responded, half-puzzled, half-amused as she uncrossed her arms and settled into her chair. "I suppose I do."

"And you speak loudly when you have an opportunity to do things your way?"

"Yesssss," she said, as she looked at me with a big smile on her face. "I might seem shy on the outside, but I'm anything but shy when I get to do things how I want."

"When else do you speak up?"

"I don't know—obviously not at work."

"Do you get to do things your own way at work?"

"Totally," she quickly responded. "My boss trusts me implicitly."

"I can see why you feel frustrated. Frustration exists in the gap between what is and what can be."

"Can you help?" Lisa finally asked.

Lisa had lots of piecemeal fragments of a story swirling around in her brain. But her narrative of who she was—combined with how she was in the room—was anything but coherent. We had a mystery on our hands, and I love mysteries even more than I love superhero stories. I especially love superhero mysteries.

When faced with a mystery like Lisa's, one of the first things I co-design with my clients is a fact-finding mission to reach out to their people system to fill in the gaps in their story. But Lisa was feeling so bad about her ability to lead her team that she didn't want to talk to people or have me interview them for her yet. It happens and is totally under-standable. It requires a lot of vulnerability to put yourself out there like that. We instead figured out a plan to do the next best thing in the interim—a research project of a different kind, using a streamlined, repeatable approach I developed to uncover identity narratives with or without data from the outside world.

First, we would unpack her story to see if it was any good. Then we would mine her past and her present to see what themes emerged. We would then take those themes and combine them back into a singular, cohesive narrative. And once we had that story, we would figure out how to use it for Lisa's benefit going forward.

When Lisa and I unpacked her story—separating fact from fiction—as I expected, we were missing a lot of data. She knew that she was not speaking up, that her boss was disappointed in her performance and ability to lead, and that her team was taking too long to get work done.

Lisa was disappointed, frustrated, and scared. We had a cliff-hanger or a tragedy. So we set out to fill in the gaps.

To fill in the gaps in Lisa's story, we needed to break apart three stories: her origin story, a peak experience from childhood, and a more recent peak work experience. Then, when we had all those little pieces out in the open, we could see what we had, what themes emerged, and then put the pieces back together into one coherent story. Once Lisa was clear on what her story was, she could figure out what to do with it.

Mining Your Origin Story

The first story to break apart is your origin story—the tale of how you became a superhero. But "origin story" doesn't mean the nicely polished and sanitized version you proudly roll out whenever someone asks you to introduce yourself. The origin story you're looking for is a messy ramble that answers the broad question: How did you get into what you do? It should answer questions like:

- What were your goals?
- What motivated you?
- What called you to action?
- What actions did you take?
- What got in your way, internally or externally?
- What *could* have gotten in your way?
- How did you overcome your obstacles and meet your goals?
- Did you do it alone or with other people?
- And ultimately, what kind of impact did you have or are you having? This impact can be on you, on other people, or ideally on both. It's tangible, and it can involve thoughts, metrics, emotions, or ideally a combination of all these.

When Lisa told me how she got into her line of work, we learned that she had a meandering career path that led her from volunteering at her college radio station to working at nonprofits. She eventually landed at a civic tech startup as a web content writer and producer, and worked her way up to senior leadership roles overseeing digital strategy and content.

What motivated her on this journey was the desire to create new ways for the public to connect with information and services that could make their lives better. Lisa was inspired by this mission, and she was determined to make it a reality. It's what kept her on track as she navigated messy situations with ever-changing work goals and responsibilities, and the kind of strong personalities who tend to inhabit both startups and nonprofits.

Lisa leveled up quickly, first as a manager and then as an executive—a pathway she neither expected nor planned for. Her first promotion came when her boss suddenly left to take a job with the Obama administration, leaving Lisa to take over her team and department without any preparation. She got her next promotion when her executive director didn't have the funds to hire a seasoned Silicon Valley executive and thought that Lisa would be a great head of digital (she was).

Finally, she was promoted into her current position when her organization unexpectedly received a multi-million-dollar grant to build out its tech capacity so it could better meet its public service mandate. In each situation, she thrived in ambiguity as she created new teams, processes, and ways of working that moved her organizations forward.

While Lisa never planned most of this career path, doing the work she did made her incredibly proud. But it also made her incredibly anxious. Anxiety, shyness, and not believing in her organization's mission were the biggest things that could or would get in her way. They were her kryptonite. (More about the dangers—and opportunities—of kryptonite in Chapter 4, "Manage Your Kryptonite.") But Lisa was determined and relished leadership roles where she could work toward a greater good.

How did she get past her shyness and anxiety? She relied on her determination. This strategy sometimes worked, but not often enough.

Mining Your Peak Experiences

The second story Lisa and I unpacked was one of her peak childhood experiences—a project, activity, or time when she felt at her best and completely excited and alive. When you mine your own peak experiences, you want to cover these kinds of questions:

- What were you trying to achieve?
- What called you to action on the project—was it an opportunity, something you saw could happen, something you initiated, something someone asked you to do, a request, an order?
- What actions did you take?
- What got in your way, internally or externally?
- What could have gotten in your way?
- How did you overcome those obstacles and meet your goals?
- Which ones did you just let rest?
- What kind of an impact did you have—not just what were you trying to achieve, but what impact did you end up having?

One of Lisa's favorite memories from her childhood was creating a rock band camp for girls in high school. One of her friends came up with the idea and asked Lisa and a mutual friend to help organize and run the camp with her. Lisa was a drummer who played in rock bands, and she loved the idea of providing young girls with the tools they needed to do the same. But she had no idea how to organize or run a camp.

Digging into the challenge, Lisa found a few people across the country who had started their own rock camps, learned from their successes and mistakes, and eventually came up with her own camp model. It wasn't easy. But she was extremely motivated by this mission and energized by innovating on what other people had done.

As a drummer, Lisa was no stranger to stage fright, and this anxiety extended to her new role as a camp director who had to be on stage a lot. But her mission and her close relationships with her bandmates—and now fellow camp directors—helped her feel more calm, clear, and focused when she was in front of crowds giving speeches or in meetings with donors asking for money. It also helped her when donors were skeptical of her unorthodox approach to, well, everything. She always knew that if anything went wrong, she was not alone.

The rock camp for girls was a huge success. Lisa rarely saw women on stage playing in a rock band. She was excited to help give young girls in her hometown the knowledge and the courage they needed to play in and start their own bands.

When Lisa recounted her third and final story—a more recent peak work experience—the themes of mission-building, determination, relationship-building, navigating messy situations, and doing things her way started to emerge more clearly.

Lisa's favorite work project was an app she had helped create a few years earlier. The app aggregated census data, enabling anyone to visualize and export that data to use on public service projects. She was invited to lead the project by a former colleague who trusted her implicitly to innovate what other organizations had done before. They had become good friends over the years, and Lisa trusted him to have her back when she needed it.

The project was underfunded and understaffed, but Lisa was driven by her mission to empower people by giving them the tools they needed to learn and communicate. She also loved that she got to do things her way rather than taking orders. Absent this level of autonomy, Lisa wouldn't have enjoyed working on the project because it was quite messy. Lisa's colleague knew that about her and gave Lisa just enough flexibility—yet just enough support—to do her thing, and do it well.

Lisa managed a diverse set of stakeholders—both internally and externally—and a diverse set of impassioned expectations and constraints from engineers, product managers, public officials, and donors. It was scary and hard at first, but it got easier over time as Lisa got to know everyone better. As she did this, she became more comfortable sharing her unorthodox solutions and getting people to trust her hunches.

"That was a lot of talking," I said with a smile after Lisa recounted these stories.

"Yeah," she answered. "I have no problem talking when people ask me questions."

"I know. Responding to a purpose-driven request is one of your superpowers."

"That does sound like me. How did you know that?"

"Because you told me."

"Did I? I didn't notice."

Lisa did not notice how much speaking up she did when she was using her superpowers. A lot of us don't notice how well things work when we are living our best stories. We only notice them when they break—when we break.

Putting It All Together

After Lisa unpacked her stories, it was clear that she was motivated by a challenge that came in the form of a request. Some people I work with are different—they are more motivated by an opportunity that they identify, and they bristle at requests. That's why it's good to know what calls you to action—no two superheroes are the same.

But the kind of request that motivated Lisa couldn't just be any request—it had to enlist her in a mission that she cared about. When she worked on the census data aggregation app, for example, the mission was to create new ways for people to get the tools they need to communicate effectively with the world around them. It not only motivated her, but it also helped her stay high level and lead her team effectively. This is important if you want to be an effective leader. I work with some folks who are motivated by solving small problems rather than big-picture problems. They usually realize that they're not cut out for leadership and are happier as individual contributors where they can exercise this super-power while letting others own the vision and mission.

Lastly, Lisa was an expert at managing and navigating messy situations, so long as she got to do things her way, and as long as she had close relationships with the people she worked with.

When she had all these pieces in place, speaking up was not an issue. It was such a nonissue that she didn't even realize how clearly and confidently she could speak when she had the necessary preconditions in place to do so.

"How does your story sit with you when you hear me tell it to you?" I asked Lisa after I repeated the CliffsNotes version back to her.

For the first time since we started running through her stories, she got quiet again.

"It's fine, I guess," she said softly, after a long pause.

"You're being awfully quiet," I said with a gentle smile, after what felt like an eternity. It was not a critique, but an observation. "What's going on?"

"This all makes me very anxious."

"I know you get very quiet when you're anxious. What's making you anxious?"

"Something's not right with this story. I see that I can speak up when I have these preconditions met. But what if I don't want to speak up?

For example, my boss wants me to be louder in meetings with our engineers. Honestly, they intimidate me."

"Did you speak up when you didn't want to at Rock Camp or on the census project?"

"No. If I really think about it, I only spoke when I wanted to. I mean, did I want to schmooze at parties or give speeches in front of large audiences? No. But did I want to inspire people to donate or share our successes? Of course."

"It sounds like that's another important piece of your story. You only speak up if you feel motivated to do so."

"Can I really do that?"

"Why not? It's your story. You get to make up the rules. It's a good thing that's one of your superpowers."

"I guess it is," she said with a big smile on her face.

At this point, Lisa and I had a very good first pass at what her real story was. But knowing is not the same as believing. Only when you truly believe your story can you fully own it and bring it to life more deliberately and in more situations. And to fully believe it, you've got to try it out, experience it, and see how it feels—mindfully.

To test-drive and stress-test her story, Lisa came up with an experiment that she would try in two different work meetings the next day. She wanted to sit back and observe how often she spoke, when, and why. One of the meetings was with two of her direct reports—Mina and Travis, whom she did not yet know very well. The other meeting was with her boss.

"What if we try the experiment right now?" I offered. "It will only take about 30 seconds."

This is a technique that I learned when I originally trained with Gestalt therapists and coaches who like to author playful experiments to try in the here and now to test hypotheses and ideas. It's also a concept that Lisa was familiar with from the tech world. We like to build prototypes to run quick experiments that test risky ideas before wasting lots of time, money, and energy building the wrong thing. Then, as we gather data, we run progressively higher-fidelity experiments—digital proto-types or A/B testing features on a live website, for example.

I asked Lisa to imagine that she was in the meeting with Mina and Travis, and to picture herself speaking a lot. "How does that feel?" I asked.

"I feel nervous!"

I then asked Lisa to imagine herself speaking a lot during the meeting with her boss.

"I feel fine," she said.

"What's the difference?"

"I don't know Mina and Travis well enough to feel comfortable, I guess," she answered, validating a core part of her story.

Next, I asked her to imagine that she was in the meeting with her direct reports, but this time she knew more about them—the name of one of their dogs or kids or hobbies—anything. Then I asked her to imagine what would happen if she knew those things and spoke more.

"As long as I imagine that I have a purpose and I want to, that feels totally fine. But it's not an important strategy meeting. We're just meet-ing to discuss something mundane. I can't always connect every little meeting to my big-picture mission and purpose. I think I'd exhaust myself," she continued as she got quiet again. Lisa didn't seem as anx-ious this time. However, I could see that she was thinking.

"What if I decided to make the primary purpose of the meeting to get to know Mina and Travis better? Do you think that would make me feel more comfortable talking with them?"

"Let's try right now."

We iterated our experiment and continued with the roleplay.

"I think I can do this" she said after a moment with that confidence and clarity she had when she could do things on her terms and with purpose. "When I imagine my purpose is to get to know Mina and Travis tomorrow, I can imagine myself talking a lot. But not for the sake of talking. I mean, who wants to hear their boss talk just to hear themselves? I can see myself asking questions and them asking me questions. I can see us having a great conversation and then also getting work done."

"How do you feel when you tell me that?"

"Excited. Nervous. Motivated."

When Lisa tried this little experiment in her meeting with Mina and Travis the next day, it wasn't easy. Taking your new story out for a spin never is. She started the meeting by asking them how their weekend was. It felt forced and awkward at first, which made her feel extremely anxious. And as she became more anxious, she noticed that she got quiet again. But the approach gave Mina and Travis enough space to tell Lisa about their weekends. Anxiety is a useful emotion in small doses.

Lisa found out that Mina had a dog named Butter and that Travis was a pinball champion. The more she learned about them, the more she relaxed. As she eased into the conversation, Mina and Travis started asking Lisa questions about her. The next thing she knew, they were all chatting about puppies and video games, which Lisa was easily able to maneuver into talking about their project.

She had a purpose for this meeting, after all. Lisa discovered that when she was relaxed enough and energized enough, running the meeting felt effortless. Instead of being paralyzed by anxiety and shutting down as she had in the past, she was engaged—and engaging.

"I just ran a meeting where I felt relaxed *and* energized at the same time!" she texted me later that day. "And all I had to do was talk about puppies!" I knew that Lisa loved dogs, so I took that as a good sign.

"How did it go?" I texted back, including a few puppy emojis for good measure.

"I owned that meeting. But it didn't feel natural at all, though."

"It rarely does at first."

"Will it ever?"

"There's only one way to find out."

When Lisa came back to see me a couple weeks later, she was excited to share what she'd learned by trying her strategy out with more people. She found that asking people about their weekends was too prescriptive and formulaic. In the end, it demotivated her. Since she only wanted to speak if she felt motivated to do so, this wouldn't work in the long run. But since she liked doing things her way, she decided to figure out a better way to connect with people. For example, she tried instead to initiate conversations at the beginning of her meetings by asking people what they were watching on TV that week. It felt easier, less forced, and made her feel less anxious. She experimented with a few other topics, and in the process realized that it didn't matter what she talked about. She was connecting with her colleagues, she felt motivated, and they were getting work done as a result.

In the weeks that followed, Lisa used her prototype as a blueprint for bigger experiments as she got to know more people inside and outside her organization. She was embarrassed to realize that she didn't know many people very well, but she was glad she had figured this out. As each meeting got less and less awkward, she felt more and more powerful.

Over the next year, Lisa stopped trying to speak up entirely. She just let herself be herself. The more she did that, the more she spoke—but that wasn't the point. The more she was herself, the more engaged she was. The more engaged she was, the more everyone else was engaged. The more engaged they all were, the more effectively Lisa was able to lead herself and her organization forward. Ultimately, that's what she and her CEO wanted.

"What did you do to her?" I remember Lisa's CEO asking me when we reconnected the following year to see how things were going. "She's like a new person," he continued as he proudly recounted what they had accomplished over the last year.

That's how stories work when they're the most powerful. You don't have to tell them. You have to be them. Over and over and over again. In doing so, they become a core part of who you are, how you show up, and how you make an impact. If you do this well, other people will tell your story for you.

II

Superpowers

With great power there must also come—great responsibility.

—Spider-Man, *Amazing Fantasy No. 15*

3

Activate Your Superpowers

The Pixar movie, *The Incredibles*, is about a family of super-heroes in a world where superheroes are not allowed to use their superpowers. Early on, we're introduced to Bob Parr, aka Mr. Incredible, the family's patriarch. He works at an insurance company during the day, trying his best to be what the world expects of him. He's miserable, terrible at his job, and is so frustrated that he secretly fights villains at night to find any chance he can to use his superpowers. This isn't enough. When he can't take it any longer, he inadvertently uses his superstrength to throw his boss through a wall in a fit of anger one day, which gets him fired.

This is a trope in superhero stories: When you can't exercise your superpowers, you can't fight villains or accomplish your mission. As a result, you get depressed, angry, or frustrated. You're not at your best. And you often create problems for yourself. Being a great leader is much the same. You are at your best and do your best work when you use your superpowers: your strengths, skills, values—all the things that empower you to show up and make a difference. But as my client, Maya—an extremely talented COO of a fast-growing tech startup—learned, this isn't always an easy thing to do.

Maya often got stuck in a rut. She would spearhead a new initiative or discipline for the company—for example, a community engagement practice—learn how to do this, fix all the problems, and grow a new team. She worked quickly, effectively, and was inspiring to watch and work with at these times.

However, she would then forget to hire someone to manage the new team. And she would eventually slow the rest of her company down by being a terrible manager and bottleneck—unreliable, slow, and cranky. She and her team grew overwhelmed and frustrated by her inability to perform. This was unfortunate because, when she was at her best, she was the *exact* opposite, which is part of how this company became so successful in the first place.

When we started working together, Maya was convinced that she had to learn to be a better manager to the three teams she managed. It's what people wanted and needed from her. But the more she tried to manage, the worse things got. It turns out that she didn't need to become a better manager—she was already a great manager when she was focused, energized, and doing what she loved. She just had to identify her superpowers, make sure she used them to the best of her ability, and delegate the rest.

When I first brought up the notion of leveraging her leadership superpowers rather than harping on what might be broken and trying to fix her, Maya rolled her eyes. "Oh, God, not you, too," she moaned. "Can't you just teach me new management skills? Clearly, I'm missing something, right?"

Since her first job in tech, Maya had been asked about her superpowers in interviews, performance reviews, manager one-on-ones, team-building exercises, and company retreats. The intent was well-meaning. But her answers never changed anything. "I'm a strategic thinker," she'd answer. And nothing would change. Or she'd take an online test, get a list of words attributes that didn't mean much to her. And that would be that.

At one company she worked at, her co-workers even identified her superpowers for her—a data-driven twist on the traditional 360-degree review where your peers, direct reports, and manager assess your performance. Her top superpower? Attention to detail. Maya was not sure how others saw this in her, but this was not her superpower. Yet this superpower wrote her story for her as her boss continued to assign Maya projects that she hated and failed to complete. The more she protested, the more her boss reminded her of her superpower. She did not last long at this job.

But now, Maya was the boss. And something was amiss.

How Superpowers Work

Superpowers are not just a silly metaphor or nice to have. When leaders come to me with an issue like Maya's, the issue is not primarily that they lack leadership skills or need to fix some other fault or deficit. It's that they're not leveraging their superpowers.

The idea of leveraging your strengths at work rather than fixing your weaknesses is not new. Organizations such as Gallup and the VIA Institute on Character, and their flagship StrengthsFinder and VIA Character Strengths assessments, have years of data that show the business impact of using individual strengths at work. When people are allowed and encouraged to use their strengths, they are not only more confident and engaged in their work, but they are also healthier, earn more money, and have overall better well-being, a catchall term that psychologists use to assess, well, all the things.[1]

This terminology translates into tangible, systemic business results more broadly. Superpowers that start with you can have a huge impact on your business. According to Gallup, organizations with strengths-based cultures have 29 percent higher profits, 19 percent higher sales, 72 percent lower attrition, and 7 percent higher customer engagement.[2]

Strengths power people and people power businesses.

1. Tom Rath, *StrengthsFinder 2.0* (Washington, D.C.: Gallup Press, 2007) and Ryan Niemiec and Danny Wedding, *Positive Psychology at the Movies: Using Films to Build Character Strengths and Well-Being*, 2nd ed. (Newburyport, MA: Hogrefe Publishing, 2013).
2. CliftonStrengths for Organizations: www.gallup.com/cliftonstrengths/en/253808/cliftonstrengths-for-organizations.aspx

If Maya wasn't using her superpowers, she would not only be unhappy and underperforming—but she would also have a systemic impact across her organization. This wasn't some silly exercise I was suggesting.

When you're clear about the big-picture story of who you are, where you've been, where you're going, and what has motivated you throughout your journey, you'll see key strengths, skills, and values featured throughout your story. Those are your superpowers. They're what move you forward—all the things that power you and those around you to move forward.

You might find your superpowers at the beginning of your story—for example, how you get called to action on your journeys. Uncovering opportunities or responding to requests are two superpowers that a lot of leaders have. You can find them by looking at the end of your story—the outcomes you've brought about and the impact you have. And you can see them at your story's climax—when you solve and resolve problems and meet your goals. Your superpowers are what kick-start you, call you to action, motivate you to keep going, determine what you value, and create value for you along the way.

When we deconstructed and reconstructed Maya's core identity narrative, we got clear on what her superpowers really were and why they mattered. Neither strategic thinking nor attention to detail figured heavily. Her story was simple and more straightforward: She loved to learn new things and fix problems. These are both tremendous assets at startups and messy tech companies, where everything is new and there are many problems to fix.

When she saw something broken or an opportunity to make something better, Maya set out to fix or improve what could be better. No wonder she was always trying to fix herself. She did so by learning new things and building strong relationships with the people she worked with. She was a lifelong learner and loved to jump in and try new things whenever possible. When she did this, she felt focused, energized, and curious—all things that kept her engaged.

When Maya encountered challenges along her journey or felt stuck, she could usually rely on one of the people she had a relationship with to help her out. But there was another instance where she tended to flounder that she never figured out how to get past. When she had completed what she set out to do and then had to manage and maintain the systems she created, she was a terrible manager.

But Maya wasn't always a terrible manager. When she was learning and fixing things, she was an excellent manager. When she was in maintenance mode and no longer learning new things or improving things, she was a terrible manager. Just like most superheroes, Maya did her best work, and felt best, when she was engaged.

As we homed in on Maya's top three superpowers—learning, fixing, and building relationships—she was surprised and embarrassed.

"How did I not know this already?" she asked as she furrowed her brow, crossed her arms, and slouched back into her chair. "I should know this by now, right?"

What we uncovered were not just superpowers—but superpowers with a story. As such, they were even more powerful than they were on their own. And they took a lot less time to find than taking an online test. Stories engage and inspire you. Facts, figures, and reports do not.

"Can I do this for my team?" she asked.

"Yes," I answered. "The more super they are, the more super you will be. But you already know that, don't you, Superman?"

Maya laughed and smiled for the first time in a long time. My joke was terrible—that's one of my superpowers.

Before Maya could go about helping her team uncover and develop their superpowers, however, she had to finish her story. What she had was otherwise a cliff-hanger.

It was now clear that managing and maintaining the systems she built were not things that Maya wanted or needed to do, and in fact, they made things worse. Hiring and delegating those tasks had been on her to-do list for a long time, but she never found time to focus on them.

With renewed perspective and potential energy to guide her, she left our session that day with a clear mandate: create a hiring plan and start putting it into action. Unlike the other times she tried to prioritize hiring and delegating, this time she was actually motivated to do it. She could see the full story of what was and what she could be.

The only problem was that as motivated as Maya was, hiring and delegating involved fixing and relationship-building, but not a lot of learning. Would she get bored? Give up? Move too slowly because the task felt tedious? Normally, when faced with a daunting task or challenge, you want to figure out how to leverage your superpowers to motivate yourself to do great work. In this case, however, Maya couldn't think of a way to incorporate learning into this last stretch of her journey.

Maya decided to track how she felt about her task at hand as she progressed and figure out what to do if she ran into any problems. If she started to feel cranky, tired, or just unmotivated to move forward, she would check to see if she was exercising her other superpowers. If so, she would figure out how to add some kind of learning experience into this project—a new hiring philosophy, new software, something more about her human resources business partner—*anything*.

When I next saw Maya a couple weeks later, she was a different person. Her grimace and furrowed brow were replaced with a beaming smile and eyes wide open. She was Maya with her cape—*SuperMaya*. Over the previous two weeks, she created a new role, found the budget, and started hiring a manager to take over the community engagement project and team that no longer needed her. She even learned more about Lance, her HR VP, and his hiring secrets, which helped motivate her when she felt stuck.

Within a few months, Maya transformed her organization from one where she was a managerial bottleneck to one that was a well-oiled system. She did so by activating her superpowers and reminding herself to use them when she felt stuck.

Finding Your Superpowers in Your Heroes

Superpowers are best used when you're in trouble, facing a challenge, on a mission, or have an opportunity to make a difference. But sometimes you don't have time to reconstruct an entire identity narrative to uncover them.

A quick-and-dirty way to find your superpowers or make the ones you already have even more powerful is to find them in your heroes. They can be people who are living or dead, your favorite boss, or someone you've never met. They can be friends, family, colleagues, celebrities, someone in the news, someone who is politically active, someone who has made a difference in the world, anyone. Who you choose to admire tells you more about yourself than the other people.

I often do this exercise when I facilitate workshops where we don't have time to delve into full identity narratives and pull strengths out of that. And I sometimes use it with clients when we want to add extra depth and memorability to their core story and superpowers we have already identified.

Start by identifying three of your heroes and then identify what characteristics you admire most about them. That's it. Those are your superpowers. If you have uncovered your story in other ways, you'll see the overlap.

For example, three of my heroes are Dolly Parton, Eleanor Roosevelt, and filmmaker, Agnès Varda. When I look at what I admire most about each one of them, and then combine these qualities together, they coalesce to form the perfect protagonist for my story, which features the things I admire most about them throughout the story.

For example, Dolly is a successful serial entrepreneur and business owner—she has an uncanny knack for seeing opportunities to blaze trails and make a difference in people's lives. Her Dollywood theme park became the largest employer in Sevier County, Tennessee[3]— where she was born into rural poverty, like many of the people whom she now employs—and she created the Imagination Library which has gifted more than 176 million free books to children around the world, inspired by her father who never learned to read.[4]

When Dolly sees a story that's waiting to be written or needs a better ending, she writes it. Not just with songs. But through her beliefs, actions, and business and nonprofit enterprises.

That's pretty cool. Those are superpowers that I have, too, and need to remember to use more often.

Eleanor Roosevelt was concerned with helping the world be a better place. According to historian Blanche Wiesen Cook, "Eleanor Roosevelt did things that had never been done before. She upset race traditions, championed a New Deal for women, and on certain issues actually ran a parallel administration" to her husband, President Franklin Delano Roosevelt.[5] She did so by embracing an incredible, if not uncomfortable, opportunity as a public figure.

Roosevelt was shy and lonely as a child and didn't love public attention as an adult, but she knew it was the best way to make an impact. This trait could have gotten in her way, but it didn't. She set out to earn as much as FDR in her first year as First Lady, and met her goals through speaking, writing, and commercial broadcasts. (She donated much of the money to charities.) Oh, and she was a mom. With six kids! Most of this was not typical for a woman to do then, nor is it typical today.

3. www.eteda.org/data-library/major-employers/largest-employers/
4. https://imaginationlibrary.com/about-us/
5. Blanche Wiesen Cook, *Eleanor Roosevelt*, vol. 2, *The Defining Years, 1933–1938*, reissue (New York: Penguin Books, 2000).

But it's not just *what* she did that I admire, but *how* she did it. Much like Dolly when she played a supporting role on *The Porter Wagoner Show*, Roosevelt did her best work initially in the shadow of someone else before stepping out on her own.

As an executive coach, I, too, do my best work in the shadows while supporting my clients to make a huge impact in the world. And when I need to, I step out, take a public role as a speaker, writer, business owner, and activist so that I can make an even greater impact. It's not easy. Like Roosevelt, I'm shy and awkward and would rather not put myself out there. But just like a good superhero, I know my purpose and use my superpowers to get the job done, whether it's as a coach, business owner, speaker, writer, or mom. Often, all of the above.

The filmmaker Agnès Varda was a founder of the French New Wave film movement in the mid-1960s. She was a trailblazer in an industry that didn't (and still doesn't) have many women filmmakers. Through her narrative and documentary films, she saw the beauty in the everyday world around her, and she uncovered things lurking beneath the surface and presented them to the world—encouraging people to look at things differently and think about things differently with an uncanny combination of reverence, lightness, and humor.

Those are superpowers I used as a documentary filmmaker and especially use today as a coach, writer, and keynote speaker. It's my job to see things that people cannot see. As long as I share what I see, I inspire people to think and work differently. When I combine that with idealism and perseverance, I'm at my best and most powerful.

That's my story, as told through the lens of what I admire most about my heroes. And those are my superpowers featured throughout.

When I encounter an opportunity or challenge, I'll sometimes ask myself, "What would Dolly do?" I didn't originate that phrase—Dolly Parton has many admirers who have asked the same question—but it's important to me. It's not about, how should I do my hair that day? If you know what I look like, I look nothing like Dolly Parton and I don't ever plan on looking like her. But it just reminds me to get out of my head when I feel stuck and get perspective on how I can overcome a given challenge whenever I feel stuck. It's as powerful as a kid putting on a Batman suit and feeling super, according to psychologists.

What would Dolly do in this case? Ah, she would advocate for her vision that everyone is saying is nuts with a wink and a smile. OK, I can do that. And if I combined my heroes into one superhero, what would she do? She'd activate her curiosity like Agnès, her empathy and perseverance like Eleanor, and she would advocate like Dolly—all while blazing paths from the shadows and in public like all three.

Phew. Not bad. I've gotten out of many a pickle—and the occasional existential struggle—by letting my heroes remind me of my superpowers. And so can you.

TRY THIS

What are your superpowers? What keeps you going and what ultimately helps you make the impact you want to make? You can see these in your core identity narrative or your heroes.

Next, think about a challenge from your past where you felt afraid, frustrated, or stuck. Go back as far as you like. And use work, life, or family as your canvas. Recall how you used your superpowers to overcome that challenge. How did your superpowers serve you? What did it feel like to use them? How have your superpowers not served you, or how have they gotten you into trouble when you used them too much? What did that feel like? What do you see? What stands out to you?

Consider this story as a prototype for how you can use your superpowers to overcome challenges in the future. Do this for as many challenges or past stories as you like. You likely have many.

Now, think about a current challenge you're having at work or in your life. Choose one or more of your superpowers and imagine how you can use them to overcome your challenge. What feelings come up for you as you imagine using them? What comes up for you as you imagine overcoming this challenge?

Add some tension here to make this story better: imagine what could happen if you overuse your superpower or superpowers. What does that look like? Feel like? If you're struggling with imagining the future, feel free to visualize this either in your mind's eye or on paper.

Whatever you come up with is a great first draft, and as such, it can be a prototype or a blueprint that you can use and iterate and move forward with throughout your journey.

4

Manage Your Kryptonite

I n 1943, the team behind the *Adventures of Superman* radio show, which ran alongside the popular comic book series, had a conundrum. Their production schedule was grueling and didn't leave a lot of time for breaks. The show's voice actors, however, needed to rest between performances. To accommodate this, they used a plot device to take Superman out of commission for these much-needed breaks. The device was called *kryptonite*—an alien element that weakens Superman.[1]

---

1. www.dc.com/blog/2018/04/05/the-weird-and-wonderful-history-of-kryptonite

Over time, kryptonite has become a part of the common vernacular to refer to anything in daily life that has the power to weaken or lead us to failure.[2] Kryptonite gets in the way of us being super, and it especially gets in the way of leaders making an impact.

When your kryptonite at work is as straightforward as classic kryptonite is for Superman, it's easy to manage. For example, the kryptonite for a lot of teams I work with is too many meetings. They do everything in their power to avoid them. They inventory, assess, remove, shorten, or rethink meetings entirely. This is smart. It's best to avoid or limit what makes you weaker.

Sometimes, however, your kryptonite exists in a gray area—partly situational, partly a characteristic, behavior, habit, or fault that makes life difficult or holds you back from doing important things. For example, having to schedule meetings with other people is my kryptonite—not meetings, just scheduling. It lowers my energy, distracts me from high-level thinking that is essential for running a business, and is something I do not do well. As an executive coach, however, I facilitate meetings for a living. And I'm that rare introvert who loves meetings. I do my best work in meetings. Avoiding meetings is not an option for me.

For straightforward kryptonite-like scheduling, I've got straightforward options. I can learn to get better at scheduling things by reading books about time management, project management, or taking a course. Or I can automate, delegate, and avoid rescheduling when possible. I prefer the latter. I rely on online calendars, automated invites, assistants, collaborators, and a fine-tuned, time-blocked schedule that I spent years developing with friends, colleagues, and coaches. (Working alone is also sometimes my kryptonite, which is why I call in help for certain things when I need to.)

When I have no choice but to deal with scheduling, I accept that I will be weakened, possibly derailed, and plan accordingly. Could I get better

---

2. Oxford Languages: www.google.com/search?q=define+kryptonite and Merriam-Webster: www.merriam-webster.com/dictionary/kryptonite

at scheduling or learn how to be a better time zone coordinator? Sure. Is it worth my time? No. I'm actually great at managing my time. It's just the coordinating schedules with other people part that derails me. Sometimes it's much faster and more efficient to automate, outsource, or avoid something like this rather than trying to get better at it. Straightforward kryptonite usually has straightforward solutions.

Other times, however, your kryptonite runs deeper than something as seemingly benign as dealing with coordinating calendars or avoiding alien rocks. It runs so deep that you can't even see it. But if you know what you're looking for, you will know when it's there. And when you know how it works, you'll know what to do with it.

When the Problem Is You

Sometimes, your kryptonite is more complex than what you can simply avoid or manage. It's a personal behavior or characteristic that acutely weakens you and everyone around you, gets you into trouble, or causes problems for you. Your kryptonite is a part of you. It's you. For that, you need a different strategy.

This was the case for an executive I once worked with—who shall remain nameless to protect the innocent. This executive had the ability to collect and create chaos wherever she worked—it was some extremely powerful kryptonite that radiated outward to the rest of the organization and beyond. It was so intense that she was known in her company as the Queen of Chaos. She continuously immersed herself in the messiest situations and then got so caught up in them that she would burn out in spectacular fashion and burn others out in the process. This impacted her relationship with her partner, her kids, her CEO, and her team.

When this executive showed up for her first session with me, she was late to our appointment. "I need help," she said abruptly as she proceeded to check email, respond to text messages, and talk about anything and everything.

"Something needs to change," she continued as she moved on to the next topic.

The faster she talked at (not to) me (I didn't have much space to participate in the conversation) and the faster her eyes darted around the room, the more anxious I felt. Our conversation was like a tornado without a purpose—spiraling, meandering, and demolishing any goals or intention in its way.

I wanted to help and could understand her desire—and need—to change something. Being in her presence felt paradoxically energizing and exhausting at the same time.

"My friends call me The Queen of Chaos," she told me as she slowed down and bashfully made eye contact with me. "It's a nickname I've had since I was a kid. I'm just so scattered. I'm constantly changing my mind, changing my focus. I make everything harder than it needs to be. It's my kryptonite. I don't want to be like this anymore. I'm tired. Everyone else is tired. And I seem to be making everything worse."

An early hire with years of startup experience, she was a superstar who had risen to the top of a fast-paced, messy Silicon Valley tech unicorn by creating an organization that launched experimental products that found a high rate of market success. Things were great until they weren't. After a year of wins in this new role, she started to see out-of-control attrition, missed deadlines, and inconsistent performance in her team.

"Why does everything I touch break?" she asked earnestly before she let out a deep sigh and slumped deeper into her chair. Before I could respond, she perked up and moved on to the next thought. She was as fast of a talker as she was a thinker.

"What's going on?" I asked.

"I'm working on too many things," she continued. "I'm building my org out while working on a high-stakes initiative with our CEO, finishing my MBA, and parenting two amazing kids who barely see me. I'm a mile a minute. My team can't keep up. They're letting me down. I'm letting our CEO down. I'm letting my kids and partner down. I'm making everything worse."

"Can you give me an example?"

"I can give you 20!"

"How about just one." I countered with a smile. I wanted to engage the awe-inspiring tornado before it spun up again.

"OK. My team was working on a special project for our CTO. When we started building our proof of concept, I was clear with the team about what I wanted. Then a month into the project, I found out that one of our main competitors was working on a similar concept. So, I brought a better idea to the team. They said they'd work on it and would have something new to show the CTO in a few weeks. A week after that, I had an even better idea that I brought to the team. I know I changed my mind, and I tried not to, but it was a really good idea.

"They said they'd try it. But when I checked back in a week before the presentation, their prototype was a mess. A total mess. I had a meeting scheduled with the CTO a few days later that I had already postponed twice. He was getting annoyed with me, so I needed to keep it.

"I ended up having to spend the next week, including nights and week-ends, fixing the prototype with the team. I missed my preschooler's graduation. And for what? In the end, we delivered half of what we promised. We were all exhausted. One of our engineers quit a few months later. I'm failing as a boss. I'm failing as a parent. I'm a mess."

"I can see that you're not OK with this," I said.

"This is what I do. It's chaos. It's always chaos. Why do I do this to myself?"

"What makes you think that you caused this chaos?" I asked, genuinely curious. I work with a lot of founders and executives who create similar chaos and go for years without knowing the havoc they wreak. It often takes a trusted advisor, colleague, mentor, or investor to be the first one to tell them that there is a problem.

"My head of engineering is a good friend of mine. He flat out told me last year. I didn't want to believe it at first. And honestly, I was pissed off. I mean, come on, really? I've spent my whole life trying *not* to immerse myself in and create more chaos. Why am I still doing this? But I know he's right. He's always right."

The Queen of Chaos trusted her friend. And she tried desperately to change, which is something she had been trying to do since she was younger. She tried breathing. Yoga. Therapy. Sports. It helped a little, but not enough. Over time, this led to enforced vacations. Hiring and firing a succession of project managers and executive coaches. None of that worked. Or something would work temporarily and then she'd revert right back into her old Queen of Chaos ways.

Her inner battle was fierce. She kept fighting herself, becoming ever more erratic, and attracting and creating more chaos wherever she went. After hiring and firing two executive coaches in the same number of months, she sought help one last time. She desperately needed to change. Or find a new job.

The Paradox of Change

Many leaders I work with come to the same sobering realization as the Queen of Chaos did. As much as they try to locate the problem with their team, company, process, or products, they realize that *they* are the core problem. Then they try to change something core to who they are. When they fail to change, they revert to their old habits. Then they try again. And their story writes itself.

Superheroes wanting to change their behaviors or characteristics that hold them back is a common theme in superhero stories. They fight villains. And they often fight themselves. It makes stories more engaging. And it also makes them human.

Take Marvel's superhero, the Incredible Hulk. When his alter ego, physicist Bruce Banner, is subjected to extreme emotional stress, he transforms into Hulk—often engaging in out-of-control, destructive rampages. Or consider Elsa, from the Disney movie, *Frozen*. When we first meet Elsa, her ability to freeze people, places, and things harms people and gets her into a lot of trouble. She spends years trying to deny, circumvent, and get rid of her ability.

You can't have a hero—and definitely not a superhero—without outer or inner kryptonite. It's as much a part of being a superhero as it is a part of being human.[3] It's what makes these characters and their stories so relatable and engaging.

But what Bruce Banner and Elsa both learn is that their inner kryptonite is also where their power comes from. It's this power that enables them to defeat evildoers. To succeed, both Hulk and Elsa need to face what holds them back, embrace it, and learn how to use it for good. That's when they're most powerful. When they do that, they transform from ill-adjusted misfits to more powerfully integrated superheroes. It's not easy. They still fight themselves often, and it makes their stories even more engaging and relatable. But over time, when they can harness their inner kryptonite as a superpower and use it accordingly—not too little, not too much—they're ultimately more super.

Even Superman needs his kryptonite sometimes. It's a part of him, per se, but it's also a part of his identity and his story—it comes from his home planet and arrived with him on Earth. It teaches him a lot about himself, his background, his powers, and his limitations. And it's even situationally useful sometimes. For example, it helps surgeons operate on him—it's the only way for a scalpel to penetrate his super skin. He even gives Batman a kryptonite ring to use in case Superman is ever under mind control, dangerous, or needs to be weakened.

---

3. Ivory Madison, "Superheroes and Supervillains: An Interdependent Relationship," in *What Is a Superhero?*, ed. Robin Rosenberg and Peter Coogan (Oxford, England: Oxford University Press, 2013), 157–160.

Your inner kryptonite is powerful stuff when you figure out how to leverage it. Like it or not, it's a kind of superpower. Because like it or not, it's really strong. The best way to conquer this type of inner kryptonite isn't to fight it. It's to fully understand how it serves you so you can figure out how to properly use it. When you do that, real, powerful transformation happens.

Harnessing Your Internal Kryptonite

When the Queen of Chaos took the time to admire her superpower and see how it had served her throughout her life, she could finally see its full strength for the first time. Part of what made her ability so powerful was that it had been with her since she was a child. It was like a muscle that she had learned to flex. In the process, it got stronger and stronger. But she didn't develop this ability because it created problems. She developed it because it served her in certain situations.

For as far back as she could remember, the Queen of Chaos had lots of energy. She got excited about new ideas often, which gave her even more energy. She was constantly bouncing around from project to project and interest to interest. With this energy, she'd imagine possibilities for the future that got other people excited and engaged. This attribute gave her even more energy.

For example, she created the first competitive math team at her high school after hearing the idea from a friend across the country. She helped her college newspaper build its first ever website and digitize its catalog after learning about other schools going online at a journalism conference. And she made her family life fun with this energy by always introducing new games and activities that entertained her siblings and parents and now her kids and partner. Then she would change the rules to keep everyone engaged.

At work, it was a similar story. Early in her career, this executive was one of the first people at her early dotcom to introduce the idea of shipping apps on the web rather than on DVDs. It totally disrupted the way they did business. It was exciting. And it paved the way for her to work on much cooler things with even more amazing people and companies over the years. Web 2.0, the internet of things, Web3—the list was long. If it was interesting enough, she got excited. When she got excited, she made things happen.

When behaviors work for you, they start to function like a habit. You have an itch, you scratch it, you feel better. Stimulus, action, reward.

When the Queen of Chaos had an idea, she got super energized, and this engaged her world to bring the idea to life with her. At her best, she was really a Queen of Energy. When an ability like this produces positive results, you default to it. Eventually, it becomes such a part of you that you don't even know you're doing it. It becomes your identity. It's just who you are.

The problem, however, is that when this behavior becomes all-powerful, there is often a cost to overusing it. When you have an itch, and you scratch too much, you bleed. When you get angry, turn into Hulk, and you can't control your superstrength—you harm people. It's a story that most of us don't want to happen. It's the kind of story that owns us if we don't figure out how to rewrite it.

The Queen of Chaos was clear on the costs of overusing her strength. When she got too excited about a new idea, had too many ideas in quick succession, or was unable to effectively channel her energy to engage people, her excitement and changing whims felt like a tornado. This tornado spiraled up into the air and when it encountered a flimsy structure—like a team at work that wasn't sure about its purpose or core direction—it would engulf and tear it to pieces.

Having experienced this tornado in our first conversation, I understood its power. If it wasn't my job to keep us on track, I too could have been swept up in its vortex.

As long as the tornado was contained in its focus and duration, it worked very well for her and the businesses that she transformed. At these times, the tornado tore just enough apart so that it didn't destroy everything. It paved paths forward. It was an incredible asset for someone like this executive to have. It's why she loved her job. And it's why she was promoted in the first place.

"I think I know what I need to do," she said calmly and confidently after we unpacked her kryptonite—or superpower, depending on how you spin it.

With her new awareness, the Queen of Chaos started by having frank, vulnerable conversations with her core team about how she got work done and what value it provided. She didn't want to make their lives difficult—which made her life more difficult, in return. But she also didn't want to completely reject her ability to be interested, excited, and motivated to learn, experiment with, and try new things. She enlisted their help in figuring out how to let her bring just enough chaos to work without uprooting projects, schedules, and personalities.

To do this, they built what they called "controlled chaos" days into their project schedule. These were essentially brainstorming days where they could share and explore new ideas without necessarily acting on them. They also recommended their favorite notetaking techniques for the queen to try. That way, she could have a place to put her ideas without needing to constantly put them in middle-of-the-night emails that the team felt compelled to act on the next morning. She hated notebooks. After some trial and error, they came to a new agreement: she could email ideas in the middle of the night as long as the team understood that they were to ignore her emails. If something was important enough, she would remember to bring it up the next day. And then the team had full permission to thank her for sharing her idea and put it in a backlog for a future "chaos day" or more formal strategic planning session. It was an unconventional arrangement, but it worked.

Over time, this arrangement functioned like a release valve for the queen, as well as her team. The less ashamed she felt for her chaotic ways, the less chaotic she became. The less frustrated her team was by her chaos, the more they appreciated her energy and ideas. The less she fought herself and the more she appreciated her strength, the calmer she got. The calmer she got, the better she slept. The better she slept, the less frequently she sent those 2 a.m. emails. This new trajectory enabled her team to work with more speed and agility while stabilizing attrition and eventually meeting and exceeding their goals.

Embracing her inner kryptonite didn't just affect her work, it also affected her entire life, which then affected her work in kind. Once she was able to embrace her kryptonite rather than fight it, she started to have a sense of humor about how good she was at being the Queen of Chaos. It became an identity and a nickname—a badge that she wore with honor. The more she laughed, the more she naturally breathed, which is something she had tried for years to do in vain. The more she breathed, the calmer and more focused she got. The calmer and more focused she got, the less she was distracted by new ideas. She was still energized by them—she needed them, or she could not be super. But they did not derail her.

Ultimately, the Queen of Chaos was better able to solve problems, connect with her team, and also do the same with her partner and kids at home. This path started to feel better than years of self-imposed yoga. But also, she started to have more energy to leave work during lunch and go to yoga classes. By choice. Not because people told her it was what she needed to do. By owning her inner kryptonite, the executive found the focus energy to propel herself, her team, her business, and her family forward. It wasn't always perfect. But that's all part of the journey. After all, you still need a little bit of drama to keep things exciting.

TRY THIS

Ask yourself, what is a behavior or characteristic you want to change or do differently as a leader? If you go back to your identity narrative, you can see at the point of innermost conflict that there is inner kryptonite in there. Often, lots of it.

Then ask yourself, how does your inner kryptonite serve you? If you're having trouble figuring this out, think back to a story from your past. What did using your kryptonite do for you? What might be the reason or reasons why you keep defaulting to this behavior?

Now that you understand how your inner kryptonite works, what do you want to do with it? How can you use this power for good? What can you do if you use it too much? This is your story. You get to write the next chapter.

III

Mission

If you don't like the road you're walking, start paving another one.

—Dolly Parton

5

Backcast Your Future

W hen Greg, a rising leader at a large, multinational financial services company, started working with me, he wasn't clear about what he wanted. But he was very clear about what he did *not* want. He was on a fast, precipitous climb upward at his company, where the previous year he had been promoted to the head of product marketing for his division.

He had also just received the worst performance review of his life.

It was January, and he wanted to have a better year than the one he had just had.

"Something needs to change," he told me with a sigh the first time we met. But he wasn't sure exactly what.

Greg ran a newly formed and fast-growing team at his company—let's give them the fictional name Infiniplex—and he faced many hurdles. When he created his team two years earlier, it consisted of just him and a few close colleagues. They were superstars. The team was small, nimble, and quick to come up with and launch innovative campaigns with much success. At some point, they even figured out how to turn their pet projects into ones that supported new business lines for the company. The wins came easily and quickly.

As Greg and his team found continued success, the team grew. As the team grew, they took on more projects, more team members, and more pressure to justify their existence to the rest of the company—especially to the chief product officer, who was their biggest champion.

At first, growing the team helped them perform better and faster. But at some point, the more they grew, the worse things got. After a year of hypergrowth, the team's work quality started slipping, they missed deadlines, morale was low, and attrition was high. All of this cost the company lots of money in lost productivity as the team was forced to recruit and onboard numerous new employees. As a result, Greg's reputation in the business began to show some major cracks.

Greg spent most of his time troubleshooting issues, fixing problems, and then doing it all over again. He was frustrated. His team was frustrated. They were all feeling burned out. Something had to change.

Greg spent so much time focusing on where he didn't want to go and what he didn't want to have happen, that he couldn't see where he did want to go and what he did want to happen.

"Whatever I'm doing isn't working. I think I need help focusing or getting people to listen to me or…I don't know…" he trailed off.

I work with lots of leaders like Greg, whether they run their own company, or they lead a team, or they're in charge of a department or division within a larger company. While the details of the situations vary, the gist is usually the same: you can't get to where you want to go if you're not clear on where you're going. Focusing on where you're not going won't work. You need a mission to guide you—it's the story of where you're going, why, and how you will get there.

We see an example of this in Spider-Man—the character and the story. In August 1962, Spider-Man debuted in Marvel Comics' *Amazing Fantasy #15*. *Teenager*, Peter Parker, started his story with goals—to have a social life. After being bitten by a radioactive spider, he developed superpowers and assumed a new identity—both of which could help him meet his goals, as well as a new goal: to make money.

Parker's new goal had a noble purpose: to provide for his Aunt May and Uncle Ben who were raising him. But he was so fixated on pursuing fame and fortune that he didn't yet fully see the big picture of what he could and must accomplish. As Spider-Man, his powers were best applied toward fighting villains. His inability to fully comprehend and realize this mission wasn't just a folly early on in his story. It cost his uncle his life one day when he was killed by a criminal whom Spider-Man previously had the opportunity to apprehend but decided not to. After this devastating loss, Spider-Man eventually embraced his true purpose and aligned his mission accordingly. He became a superhero—identity, superpowers, mission, and all.[1]

When Greg and I initially dug into what was going on for him, he thought he was clear on his mission and associated vision and goals. His company had one of the most robust goal-setting systems out there, and he used it religiously. He wanted his team to perform better, he wanted to be a better leader and save his reputation, and he had very clear metrics handed to him by his boss that he needed to measure all this against. While they were all important, they were merely pieces of a much bigger story that he couldn't see yet.

1. Robin S. Rosenberg, Ph.D., *Superhero Origins: What Makes Superheroes Tick and Why We Care* (Scotts Valley, CA: CreateSpace Independent Publishing Platform, 2013).

As a leader, you want to think about the things you're going to accomplish as an epic adventure tale rather than a list of goals. If you do this right, you'll not only accomplish goals, but you'll be clear on the difference you will make when you meet your goals—for yourself, your people, your colleagues, your customers, your business, and the communities in which you do business. That's your mission—it should guide you and everyone else forward. This is how superheroes work, and it's how great leadership happens.

While comic book heroes often find their mission the hard way, as a leader you can take a play from a writer's playbook and make it a little easier. Write your story. Then make it happen. You do this by starting with a vision for the end. Then work your way back to the end from the beginning. Doing this will help you make sure that your mission is as exciting, impactful, and transformative as you need it to be. And it will help you draft a plan of action to get there—and to avoid or plan for any potential pitfalls along the way.

You backcast your future.

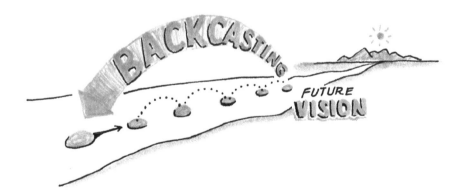

Starting at the End

The idea of kicking off a project by imagining the end is not a new idea. Backcasting is a method outlined by John B. Waterson from the University of Waterloo back in 1990. It is a planning method where you imagine a desirable future and then work backward to identify programs and policies that will connect that desired future to your present. In the business world, we simply call it a *vision*. It's the same way a lot of story-tellers structure their plots. It's what eventually worked for Greg and his team. And it's an approach that will work for you, too.

You can find your vision for your ending in one of two ways: you can dream big and make it up. Or you can use real data—quantitative and qualitative—such as business analytics, stakeholder or customer research, conversations with your team, your past and current experiences, dreams, and desires. Ideally, you use a combination of all the above.

When I realized that neither Greg nor I was clear on his mission, this is what we did.

"Will you try something with me?" I asked Greg.

"Maybe," he responded.

"Imagine it's a year from now. You've had the best year of your life. You're taking some time to tell me about the year you've had. What would you be telling me? What's better? What's different? What's amazing? The only thing I ask is that you answer me in first person, past tense."

"Role-playing?" he snapped as he crossed his arms in indignation and let out a deep sigh. "I hate role-playing."

"Me, too." I answered. "Humor me."

The truth is that I actually do hate role-playing. I'm shy, thoughtful, and deliberate. I find it unnatural and uncomfortable to play in this way. But when you imagine your future, you learn a lot about your present.

Psychologists call this *self-distancing*.[2] By building space in between yourself and your current situation, you're better able to increase your awareness of your feelings and distance yourself from any hidden stories you might be telling yourself that are holding you back. You can do it by putting on a Batman costume or wondering *what would Dolly do?* And you can do it for your future. It's like mining your past, only you're mining your future.

"I doubled the size of our team, tripled our revenue, and launched two new products," Greg said almost automatically. As Greg told me this, he was listless. He seemed almost bored by his answer. It was as if he were taking a test or answering routine questions at a doctor's office. "Is that the kind of answer you're looking for?" he asked.

"What comes up for you when you tell me that?"

"I don't know," he paused. "It's fine, I guess."

"You don't seem very excited."

"I'm not. Honestly, I am bored by my answer." He said before taking a long pause. "I should be more excited about this." Looking down at the floor, he continued, "I used to love my job. I was so excited to show up every day. Well, not every day. But, you know, most days. I was excited about my future—in general and at this company, what I was doing, all of it. What happened to me?"

Sometimes when a leader starts working with me, they're able to quickly articulate or explore their vision for the future when I probe them. They are usually relatively new to their job or recently started at their company. Their story is in the back of their mind waiting to be unearthed. As they describe a version of what could be, they are animated, sit upright in their seat, and are paradoxically calm at the same

---

2. E. Kross and O. Ayduk, "Chapter Two: Self-Distancing: Theory, Research, and Current Directions," *Advances in Experimental Social Psychology*, 55 (2017): 81–136.

time. As they embody their future self, they speak with the clarity and confidence of someone who really did have a great year.

When I invite them back to the present and ask how they feel about their vision, they are excited, fired up, and scared. They know there are many obstacles in their way, which is part of why they seek out my help in the first place.

And sometimes, I see the opposite. When someone is unable to articulate more than a few numbers or tasks, that's a red flag. Not only is it a bad story, studies show that you are less likely to accomplish your goals. Your mission should motivate you, feel achievable, have clear outcomes, and feel *just* difficult enough to achieve.[3] That's how the best stories work. You have goals, you have impact, and you have obstacles in your way. In the same way that you are engaged by a great TV show, book, or movie, you are at your best when you're engaged by your story. Your brain can't tell the difference between the stories you imagine, hear, see, and experience.[4] You may as well use that to your advantage.

"Can I have some time to think about it?" Greg finally asked.

"Of course," I answered. "I've got the perfect homework for you."

Give Yourself an A

In the book, *The Art of Possibility*, Benjamin Zander—founder and conductor of the Boston Philharmonic—writes about an exercise he learned to do with his students when he was teaching at the New England Conservatory. At the beginning of each school year, students would arrive extremely anxious about what was going to happen during their two-semester course in the art of musical performance. It was a very competitive environment—the students were all brilliant,

---

3. Gabriele Oettingen, *Rethinking Positive Thinking: Inside the New Science of Motivation* (London: Current, 2014).
4. "Your Brain on Imagination: It's a Lot Like Reality, Study Shows," *ScienceDaily*, December 10, 2018.

super-competitive singers and instrumentalists. But they wouldn't always do well by the end of the semester. All their anxiety and performance issues had some of them flailing—and failing. The pressure was too much.

Zander asked his wife, Rosamund—family therapist, executive coach, and coauthor of *The Art of Possibility*—what he could do to diffuse this pressure. Together, they came up with an idea: What would happen if one were to hand an A to every student from the start? And that's exactly what Benjamin Zander did at the beginning of the next class. According to Zander, "We came up with the idea of giving them all the only grade that would put them at ease, not as a measurement tool, but as an instrument to open them up to possibility."[5]

To earn this A grade, however, students would be required to do one thing. Benjamin Zander relayed these instructions to the class:

> *Sometime during the next two weeks, you must write me a letter dated next May, which begins with the words, "Dear Mr. Zander, I got my A because…," and in this letter you are to tell, in as much detail as you can, the story of what will have happened to you by next May that is in line with this extraordinary grade.*[6]

The letter Zander asked his students to write was from their future selves—giving themselves an A for the class and then imagining what that would be like, what they would do, and who they would be by the end of that journey. The letters were to be written in the past tense, and Zander explained to his students, "I am especially interested in the *person* you will have become by next May. I am interested in the

5. Rosamund Stone Zander and Benjamin Zander, *The Art of Possibility: Transforming Professional and Personal Life* (New York: Penguin Books, 2002), 27.
6. Rosamund Stone Zander and Benjamin Zander, *The Art of Possibility*, 28.

attitude, feelings, and worldview of that person who will have done all she wished to do or become everything he wanted to be."[7]

At first, Zander's students were surprised and more than a little confused by this unique approach. "What do you mean?" some of them asked. But in the end, the results were phenomenal. According to Benjamin Zander, "The clouds of anxiety and despair that frequently shadow a hothouse American music academy perceptibly lift[ed]." His students were able to imagine the possibilities—what they could do in this class and how they could grow into the future that they created for themselves. But they not only imagined this future—many of them made it a reality.

Over the week that followed, Greg took time to imagine his future by giving himself an A. In doing so, he imagined possibilities that he could not see when he was operating from a place of obligation or resignation. Instead of numbers and goals, he saw himself in a cabin in the woods taking a much-needed vacation.

I'll let Greg pick it up from here:

> *I am hanging out with my family watching* Gremlins, *one of our favorite holiday movies. We just finished watching* Die Hard, *one of our other favorite holiday movies. I love watching movies with my kids, which is something that I used to struggle to find time to do. I am at peace and excited to go on a hike now that the movie is over.*
>
> *I had an incredible year at work. I doubled the size of my team, all while building a self-sufficient organization full of people who are motivated to not just tinker with new products, but just as excited and motivated as I am by the business side of bringing new things into the world. Everyone is highly skilled and has what they need to perform at their best. Their impact shows and*

---

7. Rosamund Stone Zander and Benjamin Zander, *The Art of Possibility*, 28.

is valued. I've learned a lot about the payments space and honed my own skills in product development, so I now feel confident in my expertise.

I also really shine as a people manager and leader, which brings me a lot of personal satisfaction. Through that leadership, I've helped us become more mature as a team with well-oiled operations, ongoing skill development, and a rigorous focus on team management.

I've found a balance between work and family that fits my life and needs, going into the office once a week for team collaboration days.

When Greg returned to see me, he embodied that mixture of excitement and calmness that I see when people are getting clear about their mission and mobilizing energy to head out on their journey. As he read aloud his version of the future, he seemed earnest, hopeful, confident, and clear.

Years ago, Gallup surveyed 10,000 people about what leaders must provide their people for them "to feel engaged and connected to their organization and their day-to-day work." According to this research, employees need to experience four basic things with their leaders: trust, compassion, stability, and hope.[8] In this moment, I experienced all of the above with Greg. As he read his story, Greg seemed authentic, heartfelt, confident, and hopeful. As I listened, I believed him, could see that he cared, and wanted him to succeed. We usually look to other leaders—bosses, mentors, thought leaders—to find those things. But you can also find it within. When you can find it that way, people feel it. Gallup calls these people followers. I call them *superfriends*—the people you want and need to engage along your journey. The first of those

---

8. Brian Brim, "Strengths-Based Leadership: The 4 Things Followers Need," Gallup, October 7, 2021.

people, however, is you. I wanted to know if what he was experiencing matched what I felt.

"What comes up for you when you tell me that?" I asked.

"Honestly, I'm surprised," he answered.

It turned out that Greg had been so focused on business metrics and expectations over the past year that he had forgotten how much tinkering and play mattered to him and his team. On the flip side, some of Greg's favorite people he had worked with since they started the team had the exact opposite problem: they were so focused on innovation that they refused to take time to consider the business value or implications of creating new things. This created a lot of friction in his day-to-day life. It stressed him out. And the more stressed he was, the more he focused on his numbers, the more pressure he put on his team about the numbers, and the more they pushed back.

"How did I not see that?" he said. It was a statement, not a question.

"What else?"

In addition to feeling surprised, Greg was delighted by the idea of adding innovation back into his day-to-day life. It's part of why he took this promotion in the first place. Likewise, he was even more excited by the idea of taking a vacation and watching movies with his kids. He was so stressed and busy that he hadn't been able do that in a while. Lastly, Greg was most excited and hopeful about the possibility of his team operating without him. He'd seen them do it before and trusted his team to figure this out. The sooner he could get them operating at the right level, the sooner he could have fun with his kids and go on vacations and recoup and sustain the energy he used to have for his job.

He was highly motivated to make this a reality.

But Greg was also skeptical, which is always a good sign.

"OK, now what?" he asked. "This all sounds good on paper…but can I really make it happen? Is that how this works? I say it and it's true?

Honestly, while this sounds great, I don't quite see how I can make this happen. I'm not saying I can't, but I just don't see how I'll do it."

Once Greg had a clear, exciting vision for the future that felt just out of reach but achievable, he had to figure out how to get there. To do that, he needed to write the rest of his story.

And...Action

Action is a key ingredient essential to any good story. Characters have goals and try to meet those goals. Not everything they try works, which is not just OK but expected and makes the story more engaging. In other words, trying and failing is all part of a hero's journey. What is essential at this point in the story is that a hero does things.

At this point, I asked Greg to catapult himself back to the future. As his future self, I asked him to take a few minutes to recall what he might have done to make his vision a reality as if it all had actually happened. To do that, he had to continue to recount his story to me in the past tense, first person. This part is more difficult for some people to do when talking out loud, so I invited Greg to take a couple minutes to write down his story. But not more than two minutes. I wanted him to aim for quantity, not quality, referencing how I used to run ideation workshops with software development teams. This was meant to be a draft of unfiltered ideas to build action into his story, not a polished essay or perfectly executable project plan. When he was done, I asked him to read this next part of his story to me.

"Well, first I need to hire, then I need to..." he started as he quickly read what sounded like a task list. The faster he read, the more bored I got. Don't get me wrong—I love task lists. But I complete tasks more effectively when I'm clear on my mission and my story, as do most people. It's what our brains crave. I asked Greg to put aside his to-do list and instead tell me his story. This is what he said:

Last January, I created a director role below mine so that I could get more support running product marketing. I also realized that a lot of people weren't really clear on our purpose—was it innovation for the sake of creating new, shiny things? Or was it traditional marketing focused on numbers and business value? Ideally, it was all the above, but we needed to get on the same page. So, I got the team together for a much-needed off-site so we could refocus and reorient around our mission.

At the off-site, it became clear to me that we also had a lot of skills gaps to fill. So, I set up a series of lunch-and-learns for the team and organized a few trainings throughout the year. I also increased our learning and development budget so that people could go to conferences or get coaching as needed. I continued working with my executive coach, so I had the support I needed to grow as a people manager and leader.

I developed ease and confidence when having candid conversations, and I had the right ones with the right people to start effecting change. I actively worked on listening to learn and giving continuous feedback, which strengthened my working relationships and team performance.

This all helped me better support Kevin [his boss] in driving focus, morale, and momentum for the product management team, which ultimately helped him *succeed.*

After Greg recounted some of the things he did as his future self, looking back, he suddenly appeared to be concerned.

"What's coming up for you now?" I asked.

"Honestly, this all makes me feel very anxious. This looks good on paper and sounds good. But I can think of a million reasons why this won't work."

"Good, now you're ready for the fun part."

Making It Hurt

I once took a seminar with Robert McKee, a screenwriter who taught much of Hollywood how to write screenplays through his classic book *Story* and world-famous seminars. At one point, I remember McKee emphasizing how important it is that a hero struggle to achieve their goals. As he explained the idea, he paced the auditorium. The more he paced, the more he digressed.

At some point, he caught himself, stopped, and looked directly at us.

"Never mind," he said. "This is all you need to know. Make it hurt!" he exclaimed as he pounded his fist in the air. "Go deep. Go dark. No conflict. No story."

There's a business technique popular in the tech world called a *premortem*. Initially developed by psychologist Gary Klein, it's a kind of backcasting exercise. Only, when you do a premortem with your team, instead, you assume that the project has failed, and you come up with the reasons why. This approach enables a team to identify what can go wrong on a project before they start it. The purpose is to minimize risk before investing significant amounts of time, energy, and money working on something that isn't going to deliver the results you're banking on.[9]

If you're a pessimist like me, the idea of spending an entire meeting talking about what could go wrong might sound delightful. The problem is that when you focus on what could go wrong, you lose sight of what can go right.[10] On the other hand, if you combine what can go right with what can go wrong—that is a good story. The best stories move people forward. That's what leadership is all about—it's about creating possibilities for a better future.

Achieving the goal you've set for yourself at the end of your quest isn't easy, nor should it be. If it was, it wouldn't be much of a quest, and it

---

9. Gary Klein, "Performing a Project Premortem," *Harvard Business Review*, September 2007.
10. In this video, Nobel laureate Daniel Kahneman discusses the merits of the premortem and why some people don't love them: www.youtube.com/watch?v=MzTNMalfyhM

would make for a lousy story. Too much conflict, and you shut down or burn out. Not enough, and you get bored, or worse yet, complacent.

Like how gravity helps you walk, conflict helps you move forward—in an engaging story and life. Without it, you would drift aimlessly or simply float away.

When Greg shot back to the future and looked back on his journey as his future self, he saw many things that scared him and could go wrong. I invited him to list the top three things that could get in his way. Once he got the hang of how this worked, he could think about his other blockers later, or as they came up on his actual journey. I asked him to briefly describe his challenges without solving them. We'd have a chance to do that in a few minutes. He refused to come up with a top three—he had four.

> *It wasn't always easy. My tendency to dive into the weeds on detail-level work often got in the way, as did my reluctance to ask for help. Day-to-day tasks and admin work drained my time and energy, but I wasn't always sure how to best delegate work.*
>
> *It was also clear that the leadership team above me wasn't aligned on a shared vision. It felt like there was always a long list of things to do, but we lacked the structure and focus to make meaningful progress, which felt frustrating and demotivating. As a result, I was often reactive to their changing needs, which not only frustrated me, but frustrated and demotivated my team.*
>
> *On a personal level, I lacked relationships across the company to remove roadblocks for my team or drive change at a higher level. I was also nervous to have difficult conversations and struggled to give feedback in a way that felt authentic and successful.*
>
> *And on an even more personal level, I'm not just a control freak, I'm a workaholic. As much as I tried not to, I worked nights and weekends and didn't get to spend time with my family like I wanted to. I'm my own worst enemy.*

Once Greg outlined what could have gone wrong, stepped back into the present, and admired his work, I could clearly see where his anxiety came from. He'd imagine possibilities one second and before he could even entertain them, he'd already know why he couldn't accomplish something. This left him in a perpetual state of immobilization. No wonder why he was struggling to accomplish, let alone see, his mission. He wanted to achieve big things (an epic story) and had many forces in his way (little stories).

At this point, however, instead of seeming anxious, Greg just looked sad. This is often the case at this point. It meant that we were onto something. Sadness is an easier emotion to work with than anxiety, which is really two emotions—excitement and fear—all wrapped into one twisted entity that functions a lot like kryptonite.

"What's standing out to you now?" I asked.

"I hoped I'd feel better by now, but I just feel sad and overwhelmed by all of this."

"Let's dig into that."

I put on my teacher hat and explained to Greg what was going on. The anxiety that Greg felt as he got clear on his mission—the same anxiety he felt in his day-to-day work—was a result of opposing forces fighting each other. It was powerful enough to block his vision in the first place, which is why he had struggled to even see the future when we first started talking about it. What he had were competing stories that were engaging his brain. All these stories swirled in the back of his mind and canceled each other out, leaving Greg exhausted and dispirited.

The stories that write your identity are the same stories that write or cancel out your ability to realize your dreams. *I'm a control freak, I'm a workaholic, leadership is not aligned, my team is demotivated.* To move forward, Greg had to figure out what part of his narrative was true, what was not, and what could be rewritten. Only then could he transform his story from one that held him back to one that would propel him forward.

When Greg and I unpacked fact from fiction, we got clear on what his story really was and could be. For example, he did tend to focus on details a lot. It was one of those superpowers that was also kryptonite—and it especially weakened his team as his meddling derailed them, damaged relationships, and messed up deadlines. All true. Administrative work exhausted him. True. It was also no longer part of his job description. True. And he didn't feel confident or competent as a delegator or having difficult conversations that involved giving or receiving feedback. True. His leadership team was not aligned. Possibly true, possibly not. He and his team were frustrated and demoralized. True.

When we unpacked the bit about his not having relationships across the company, however, this was part fact, part fiction. Having spent enough time at this company, he had great relationships with a lot of people. He still worked with some of them. But those relationships were now strained. The rest of the friends he had made over the years now worked on other teams. The truth was that he had relationships, but they weren't in great shape or were with the wrong people.

Was Greg a workaholic? Story. That is one of those ill-formed identity narratives such as *I'm a burden, I'm a quitter,* or *I'm an impostor.* The real story was a cliff-hanger waiting to be finished.

Greg loved what he did. He was also doing too many things. He had a hard time turning off. And he worked nights and weekends as a result. The more he did this, the more frustrated he, his team, and his family felt. The more frustrated they all were, the more relationships suffered. And he wasn't getting the results or living the life that he wanted.

Many of these challenges were manageable. Some were not. But they were things he had to overcome, or he would end up right back where he started: burned out, miserable, and needing to explain terrible performance reviews.

"OK, now what?" he asked, after we unpacked all this.

"Now you get to imagine how a superhero would overcome those obstacles," I replied. Greg was right. If all of those obstacles stayed in his way, he could not accomplish his goals. But with a little bit of ingenuity and strength, he could write the rest of his journey. Then we could figure out if and how to make it all happen.

Resolving Conflict

Whether you are acting alone or as part of a team, the good news is that you get to be the hero—you have the power to overcome your obstacles. For the obstacles that you cannot change, you can figure out how to accept them or rewrite your journey entirely. And for the things you can't overcome, you're much better off learning about blockers before you head out on your journey than near the end of your actual real-life journey. As his future self, here's what Greg imagined he had done to face his obstacles. To make this feel less overwhelming, he imagined tackling each obstacle, one at a time.

> With my coach, I focused on getting out of the weeds, empowering the team, prioritizing well, and asking for help when I needed it. This helped me stop myself from jumping in and trying to fix everything (an old habit). It also taught me how to better focus my time and energy, so I felt less stressed and anxious and could be more present for my team. I was also able to hire an assistant who took a lot of administrative, time-consuming tasks off my plate so I could focus on the bigger picture. This gave me the time and support to take courses, attend trainings, and join in on more project work so I could build my leadership skills, subject-area expertise, and confidence.
>
> As for my leadership team, they still mostly lack a vision and focus. But it's so much better than it was. I learned how to be

less reactive to their requests and collaborate more closely with them on at least starting to think about our big-picture vision. To do this, I had to learn to manage up and out. I did a series of workshops, coffees, lots of listening, and a little bit of doing things without permission and asking for forgiveness later. It's not perfect. But we can live with it.

One of the things that helped me the most was refocusing on my personal relationships with key people across the company. While this seemed daunting at first, knowing that I had done it before gave me the confidence and excitement to do it again. I planned an off-site for my team that had tons of social and downtime baked in to give us time to get to know each other better. In addition to strategic coffees, I made an effort to have non-strategic coffees with anyone and everyone I found interesting. This helped me stress out less and have more fun as I got to know people, saw how I could help them, and learned to enlist them in helping me if I needed it. But mostly, it was nice to get to know and re-know so many people. I forgot how much I missed that.

As for working too much, delegating more and asking for help freed up a lot of time that I used to spend working. But I also had to learn how to let go of trying to control how my team worked. To do this, I had to learn how to trust them—that's a work in progress, but it's so much better than it was the year before.

Once I also realized that I worked nights and weekends because I liked it, rather than being forced to do it, I chilled out a bit. If I wanted to work late one night, I let myself do it—and enjoy it. And then I would try to make up the time with my family as soon as possible so that I could still hang out with my kids. I used to spend so much time stressing out about being a perfect dad that when I was with my kids, I wasn't really present. Letting go of that pressure to be perfect felt liberating. I could work one Saturday and then take a day off the next week to

attend a school party. So long as my kids understood what I was
doing, and my team knew that they did not have to work off-
hours when I did, it seemed to work better for all of us.

As Greg returned to the present and sat with his vision and mission, he seemed calm and composed.

"What's coming up for you now?" I asked.

"This all sounds achievable?" he answered with what sounded like a question.

"Is that a statement or a question?"

"Both?" he answer-asked. "I honestly don't know how I'm going to do it all, or if I can do it all. But I'm kind of excited to try. And curious to see how this all plays out. It weirdly feels like a plan, even though it's not really a plan."

"It's a story," I explained.

The best stories are a kind of plan. You have a beginning, a middle, and an end. You have a protagonist who is trying to accomplish something. And you have challenges that are in their way. As a result, you have tension. Tension makes stories more engaging—not too much, not too little, just enough. It moves the story forward and moves us forward whether we are thinking, reading, hearing, watching, or experiencing the story.

"Can we turn this into a real plan?" Greg asked.

"Of course. But first, we need to go back to the ending to make sure it's as good as can be. Because nothing ruins a good story more than a terrible ending," I smiled.

It's not just what happens in a story that is important—it's how you feel and what kind of a tangible transformation you see that ultimately engages you. For that, you need to make sure that the ending you came up with at the beginning is good.

Strengthening the Ending

The best stories are about something bigger than what you want. They're about what you need and what the world needs. In any great story, there's always a lesson that someone learns, a transformation that people experience, and an ultimate impact on the hero, their community, and their world. The best stories have a "so what?" that matters at the end. They have outcomes and transformation that you can see, feel, and care about.

For example, when he transformed into a real superhero, Spider-Man's mission could have been to fight villains for the sake of avenging his uncle's death. It would have been a short story: Spider-Man wins. The end. But the best superhero stories are about creating a bigger impact that motivates our heroes—and audiences alike. As he eventually learns through some trial and error, Spider-Man's real mission is to save the day and help people. He feels better about it. And his world is a better place because of it.

In Simon Sinek's bestselling book, *Start with Why*,[11] he talks about the importance of understanding the "why" behind what you do. It motivates and inspires you—and those you lead—to action. It's an idea that has caught on in the business world. I routinely see people—leaders, executives, teams—who want to figure out their "why" for that exact reason. Yet they struggle to do so. On the other hand, these same leaders can easily answer the "so what" at the end of a story, whether it's a personal, team, or business story.

Big-picture impact and transformation like this makes stories not only complete, but also powerful, satisfying, and memorable. They connect with you because your brain is designed to see stories and experience stories everywhere so that you can learn from them and ultimately stay alive. The better the story, the more motivating the mission, and the better the outcome. For that, you need not just goals and dreams, but also outcomes and results.

When I asked Greg to jump back to the future and tell me what was better or different, he clarified his vision. He had covered some of this already, but it was important to finish the story properly so that he could fully appreciate his possibilities for the future.

> *My team loves working with me. And the teams we partner*
> *with love partnering with us. In all, we are seen as a model of*
> *how innovation and business don't just co-exist but thrive in*
> *a large company. While my team is self-sufficient enough to*
> *work without me while I am away, they feel good enough about*

11. Simon Sinek, *Start with Why: How Great Leaders Inspire Everyone to Take Action*, reprint (New York: Portfolio, 2011).

their progress to take their own vacations this year. It's some-
thing that a lot of them were too stressed to do in the past. I am
proud of our work and even prouder of my team's ability to tend
to their lives outside of work. They're proud, too. We have a lot
more energy to do great work and have the results to prove it.

My kids and partner are happy, too. We enjoy each other's
company. I no longer feel guilty working the occasional night or
weekend. We feel more connected to one another, and we're hav-
ing more fun as a result. We've moved on from only having time
to watch the occasional movie to watching an entire TV series,
like Dr. Who. *It's pretty cool.*

"And how are you feeling?" I asked him after he told me this. At this point, it didn't matter if future Greg or present Greg was answering me because it was all the same as far as his brain was concerned.

"I feel relaxed, refreshed, and energized," he answered with a surprised look on his face. "I almost forgot what that feels like."

When you think of what you do as a story, figuring out your "why" is a simple matter of cause and effect. It's a "so that." Once Greg was clear on his "so thats," he was fully engaged. He was ready to go make it all happen.

"Now what?" Greg said after a long pause.

"What do you normally do when you plan a project?" I asked. I've seen clients use their stories to come up with task lists, notebooks, Kanban boards, vision boards, Gantt charts, project plans, development plans, performance plans, roadmaps, OKRs (Objectives and Key Results), accountability groups, posters, art, sticky notes, and index cards. The format and fidelity matter less than the fact that you are making your mission and vision more real by engaging your mind, body, and heart, as well as your senses—sight, touch, hearing, even taste, or smell. The possibilities are endless.

"I need to think about it," he replied.

When Greg arrived at our session two weeks later, he told me about the notebook he had created. In it, he had outlined the key points in his story to motivate him. And he had outlined the things he needed to do over the next year, broken down by quarter and theme. For example, in his first quarter he would focus on developing relationships, figuring out the leadership team's mission, and working on core management skills, such as getting better at giving feedback and manager one-on-ones. His second quarter would focus more on applying his learnings from Q1 toward strengthening those relationships and strengthening individuals by using manager one-on-ones to help his direct reports figure out their mission and vision for the year.

He broke some bigger things into tasks—for example, going on a listening tour to develop new relationships across the company turned into identifying 20 people, sending invites, drafting questions, identifying key learnings, synthesizing findings, and creating a follow-up plan. And he built lots of flexibility into his plans because he knew that plans were more of a guide rail than a prescription. With a vision in mind, an idea of what he needed to accomplish, and an inkling of what could get in his way, he knew that he would work with precision, energy, and agility. He had years of experience to back this up.

But what Greg was most proud of was what he did to make sure that his mission wasn't just a bunch of lists and schedules—that could only motivate him for so long. He started to talk to his team and his family about what he wanted to accomplish, how, and why. In doing so, his story felt more real, and he started to enlist people to support him on his mission. It wasn't just his mission, after all. It was their mission—his family's, his team's, and his organization's. To support and remind him to stay on track, his 7-year-old son drew him the best ending to the story that he could imagine. He drew a family taking a vacation in the mountains at the end of the year. In the photo, everyone was smiling and holding hands. Greg kept this drawing on his desk over the next year as he made much of what he imagined a reality—especially the ending.

TRY THIS

Imagine yourself at some point in the future—any time frame from a project, quarter, year, or even 5, 10, or more years in the future works well for this exercise. Pick a possible future that doesn't just excite you because you can achieve it, but that excites you because it feels just out of reach—seemingly impossible.

Don't be humble: give yourself an A+.

Set the stage. Where are you? What are you doing? Who are you with? What have you accomplished? *Who* are you? Engage your senses as best you can. What do you see, hear, smell, and feel?

What are all the things you did to get to where you are? This part is straightforward. It's OK if it reads like a laundry list of actions and tasks. If you start seeing problems in your story, that's OK. Keep going. You'll have a chance to address the problems in a moment. For now, dream big.

CONTINUES ➤

CONTINUED ➤

Next, identify what did or could have gone wrong along your journey. What scared you? What derailed you? What got in your way? These can be external or internal threats, problems, or challenges. Don't worry yet about how or if you overcame these challenges—you'll tackle that in a moment. Just explore the possibilities. Let your fear guide you. So, go deep, go dark. Have fun with this one.

How did you overcome your obstacles? What superpowers did you use? What kryptonite did you leverage creatively? What superfriends did you engage along the way to support you? Who did *you* support? What obstacles were you not able to tackle?

Now you're near the end of your story, just where you started at the beginning of this exercise. You've met your goals, overcome your challenges—great! Why does any of this matter? To make sure this adventure tale is complete, you need to make sure your ending is compelling. If you haven't already covered it, what's better? What's different? What change do you see? In yourself, your team, your business, or in the world more broadly?

Take a moment to pause, come back to the present, and admire or assess your story. That's it. That's your mission—the change you want to see or be in the world and how you will make it happen. It's your compass and your roadmap. You can use it to create a project plan, a work of art, or simply keep it in the back of your mind as you set out on your journey and make this story real.

6

Choose Your Own Adventure

Growing up in the 1980s, I used to read a book series called *Choose Your Own Adventure*. It was popular then and still exists today. The concept is simple. These books don't follow a traditional, linear narrative architecture. They are designed more like a flow chart, with branching decisions and paths that create a different story, depending on the choices you make at any given turning point.

I loved these books as a child because I got to call the shots. But occasionally, I didn't like how my story was turning out. When that happened, I backtracked to where the story went off the rails, chose a different path, and got a much better story as a result. In doing so, I got to see all the threads, and I had the power to change the outcome.

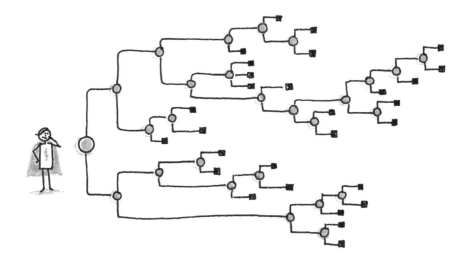

Life can work like this, too, when you prototype your possible futures before you set out on your journey and at key turning points along the way. This is what Preeti, the founder of an educational technology company, learned to do.

Preeti's Story: Version 1

Preeti and I had been working together for a while. She had plans to grow her company and was preparing to raise a round of Series B funding. That is, until one day, when she received an offer to buy her company. This unexpected offer was enticing. But it also derailed her. She felt stuck.

"I don't know what to do," Preeti admitted to me one day as she told me the news. "It's stressing me out so much that I haven't slept in days. Do I sell? Or raise another round?"

"What's keeping you from making this decision?"

"I'm afraid that I'll make the wrong decision—which won't only impact my life and my business, but it will impact everyone else, too. It's a lot of pressure. I want the company to succeed."

"Will you try an experiment with me?" I asked with a smile. Preeti had been working with me for long enough that these invitations no longer surprised her or made her feel self-conscious.

"Sure, what've you got?"

I asked Preeti to move to another part of the room and stand or sit or whatever felt most comfortable to her.

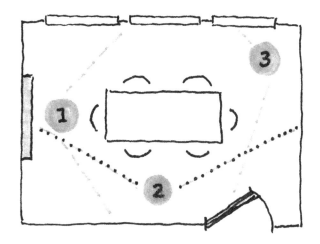

"Imagine it's five years from now," I began. When you're working on something as big as a company vision, it's better to think farther out in the future than just a year. "We're at a party and meeting for the first time. We've been chatting for a few minutes. And now I'm going to ask you one of my favorite party questions that I know is a lot of people's least favorite: *What do you do for work?* I want you to answer as quickly as possible without thinking too much about the answer. I'll then ask you more questions. We'll do this for a minute or two until we're done. Sound good?"

"Let's do this." She was ready to go.

"OK." I said as I got into character. "Nice to meet you, Preeti. What kind of work do you do?"

"I'm the chief product officer at LearningLizards."

"What's LearningLizards?"

"It makes software that helps teachers manage courses, homework, grades—stuff like that," she answered.

"Oh, cool. How did you get into that?"

"Well, years ago I founded my own company. We built online collaboration software for teachers. We got so popular that LearningLizards, a learning management company, acquired us rather than building their own collaboration features into their existing product. After they bought us, I moved into an executive role to help LearningLizards integrate our software and expand their offerings."

"What was that like? Working for yourself and then working for someone else?"

"It was difficult at first, and it took some adjustment. Merging software isn't easy. Merging cultures is even harder. I loved not having a boss, and I had to learn how to work with a boss again. But honestly, running my own company was exhausting. It's a bit of a relief to get to work on cool things with great people, worry less, and get a paycheck. It's worth the trade-off, I think."

"Cool," I said, finally. In a matter of minutes, Preeti had drafted her mission and mapped out her journey for the next five years. I invited her to come back to the present for a moment before moving on to the next version.

"What's coming up for you right now?" I asked.

"Honestly," she answered, "I don't know."

"I often don't know how I feel, either," I confided. "Feelings are hard." Identifying emotions is often difficult for technical folks, including myself.

"What's coming up in your body?" I asked. The purpose of an exercise like this is to unearth possible futures that have been in the back of your mind holding you back. The reason you do that is to figure out how you feel about those stories. Once you know how you feel, you can make informed decisions about how to move forward. But for many of us, knowing how we feel is its own challenge. When that happens, let your body tell your story.

"My chest feels tight," Preeti told me as she rested the palm of her hand firmly on her chest. Her hand was like a plate of armor. As she held down tightly, her breathing got shallower. This happens when we're anxious or threatened. Our bodies need to be ready to fight or flee at a moment's notice.

"What's up?" I asked. Preeti had been working with me long enough at this point that I didn't have to explain what happens when we feel threatened or scared.

"This does not feel good."

"What doesn't feel good?"

"The idea of working for someone else" she said before she paused for what felt like minutes. "I don't think I like it."

"Duly noted," I said. "Let's try another one."

I invited Preeti to shake her body or whatever she needed to do to step out of the future she had just embodied. I then invited her to move to another part of the room for another round. Using your body is important for an exercise like this. It engages your whole brain so that you not only unearth better ideas, but also experience them more effectively. That way, you can try them on without having to spend five years heading down the wrong path.

I've worked with some founders, for example, who took years to learn what Preeti had just learned in a matter of minutes. The more fully you experience your thoughts, the more they imprint themselves on your body.[1] For that reason, moving your body acts like a palate cleanser for your thoughts. Once Preeti was in a new spot, we were ready for Version 2.

Preeti's Story: Version 2

"Nice to meet you, Preeti. What kind of work do you do?"

"I'm the founder and CEO of a scaleup."

"What's a scaleup?" I asked, as if I had no idea what she was talking about.

"It's like a startup, but we're scaling super-fast and doubling in size every year."

"Wow, cool. How big is your company?"

"We're at 1,500 people."

"Wow, that's a lot of people."

"Yeah, five years ago we were a nimble team of 30. I never expected us to grow this fast."

"What does your company do?"

"We make remote collaboration software for teachers."

"Ah. How'd you get so big?" I asked. At this point, we had just enough of a peek into one possible version of her future—the end of her story—so I wanted to know how she got there. In this version, she still owned her company.

"It's a funny story," she said. "When I started my company, I always thought I would keep it small. It was for teachers who wanted a better way to do their job. But over time, as more people used our product, school systems started to ask us if all their teachers could use it. To

---

1. Bessel van der Kolk, M.D., *The Body Keeps the Score: Brain, Mind, and Body in the Healing of Trauma* (New York: Penguin Publishing Group, 2015).

meet the demand, we had to raise money, hire more people, and adapt our software accordingly. As we got more popular, we grew to the size that we are now. And we're going to get even bigger next year."

"Cool, it was nice to meet you." I had heard enough.

"How was that?" I asked as we took off our virtual improv hats and came back to the present.

"It's weird. I'm nervous and calm at the same time," she answered.

"Where in your body do you feel that?"

"I can feel the ground below my feet, for one," she said. "And my hands are tingling."

"If those hands could talk to you, what would they say?"

Preeti looked down at her hands for a few moments. It was as if she were holding fireballs—feeling their power and getting ready to use them. Most superheroes—including ones with names like Firestar and Sunfire—have this ability. She looked up at me and smiled.

"They'd say let's do this," she answered, clearly and confidently.

"OK," I responded, smiling in return.

When we were done, I invited Preeti to sit back down in her chair— her original position—so we could unpack what had just happened and what we had learned from a distance. Physical distance from her imagined futures gave her the perspective she needed to make sense of what she experienced so that she knew what to do about it.

"So," I started, letting her take over after she let out a long exhale.

"So," Preeti said with a smile, "I guess I'm raising another round of funding."

"How do you feel about that?"

"Scared. But the good kind of scared. I can do this, right?"

"Let's find out."

When you're excited and a little bit scared, you're usually onto something. Over the next few months, Preeti successfully raised her Series B without burning out, which was a totally different experience than when she raised money in the past. With a clearer vision of the future, and just enough fear, she had enough energy and excitement to grow her company in the way she wanted.

She would need that energy, because there were still many obstacles in her way. But it was all part of the journey.

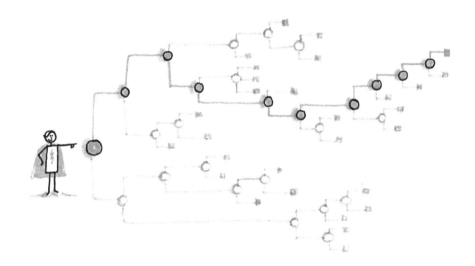

7

Tame Your Horror Stories

When my grandmother was 19 years old, she had a bad feeling. It was 1939, and the Nazis had just invaded neighboring Czechoslovakia. She was sure they would invade Poland next. My grandmother wanted to escape, and she begged her family to join her. They refused. "How bad could it get?" they asked. It was modern-day Poland, after all. Countries don't just invade and pillage other countries anymore, they argued when she first brought up her fear. As it turned out, it got bad—really bad.

After escaping with her friends, my grandmother spent the next six years as a refugee hiding in the forests of Siberia. She survived by logging trees on horseback in exchange for food and shelter. Her family back in Poland did not survive.

"Why didn't they listen to you?" I asked my grandmother incredulously, as she recounted this story to me years later. I was learning about World War II and the Holocaust in school, and I wanted to learn more.

"They couldn't see what I could see," she replied.

How Horror Stories Work

My grandmother and the rest of her family lived in two different realities. She had a keen ability to see the worst in people and catastrophize possible futures. Her family did not. Her parents and siblings couldn't fathom any other reality than the one in which they lived. They lived just outside of Lodz, a thriving, modern, integrated metropolis. They owned the one grocery store in their town that everyone—even non-Jews—frequented. At home they spoke Yiddish, a traditional Jewish language, and they spoke Polish outside of it—living in harmony with their community. Life was good. In her vision for the future, however, it wasn't.

The possible future my grandmother imagined was scary. The story that contained that vision was a scary story—a horror story, if you will. Horror stories serve the same function as all stories—they teach you something important and compel you to act. At their best, they keep you alive. But they do so in a unique way. They teach and instruct by exposing the cracks beneath the surface and illuminating what lurks in the shadows of the everyday, thereby exposing what many of us cannot or don't want to see. The best horror stories teach us about what it means to be human and how to survive. As such, they are a powerful tool to embrace rather than fear.

Unfortunately—or fortunately, depending on how you look at it—I inherited my grandmother's ability to confabulate all kinds of scary possible futures. And it's something that a lot of the most successful leaders and teams I work with regularly grapple with. The ability to foresee worst-case scenarios can be a leadership superpower when used correctly. Whether it's in the form of contingency planning, scenario planning, SWOT (strengths, weaknesses, opportunities, threats) analyses, or premortems, imagining your worst possible futures can help you avert disaster.

However, this ability to foresee scary possible futures can also petrify you and those you work with and prevent you from moving forward. As with all superpowers, it can also be your kryptonite. If you find yourself confabulating scary possible futures that stop you in your tracks, you're better off embracing this kryptonite as a superpower and using it to move you forward.

Sam's Story

By the time Sam sought out my help, she was worried. Very worried. She wanted to double her company's revenue over the next year. But she kept getting stuck.

Sam was the cofounder and CEO of a small, profitable, rapidly growing marketing technology startup. She spent most of her energy on growth—customer acquisition and revenue. Her cofounder and CTO, Dara, managed the product and engineering teams and made sure that the entire operation ran smoothly.

While the company was profitable and growing, Sam's investors and cofounder were frustrated with her. They wanted her to think big and grow the company's focus, market, and potential to disrupt the industry. Yet, she spent most of her time thinking small, changing her mind, micromanaging, and investing in the wrong areas and the wrong people. This approach not only hampered their ability to grow the company in the way that her investors wanted, but it also slowed down the company, frustrated many people, and led to unwanted attrition. They had so much potential. Yet they were hemorrhaging cash.

"Nothing I'm doing is working," Sam said to me with a sigh one day after her investor and mentor, Trevor, asked her to talk to me. "I'm working all the time, yet I don't feel like I'm getting enough done. They want me to think big and act like a CEO. How do I do that when I spend all my time working on everything?" As she continued, Sam became more animated, fidgeting vigorously with her hands. "I think I need help managing my time and delegating. Something like that. But…"

"But what?" I asked.

"I don't know. I just can't do anything right."

When people like Sam come to me for help, I first like to get grounded in their vision for the future rather than just play into their desire to solve small problems with what might be the wrong solutions. When they are trying everything, and nothing is working, the solution is rarely to try more things. It's to pause, step back, look at the future, and then figure out a path forward. But the more we talked, the more I realized that her vision for the future was exactly what was holding her back.

"What's wrong?" I asked.

"Why do I keep doing this?" she asked as she continued to answer her question. "I turn 40 next year. I should have figured this out by now. I can't work for anyone else, yet I obviously suck at being my own boss. I live paycheck to paycheck. I still rent, and I don't see how we'll ever be able to buy a place. I'm going to end up just like my dad."

"Tell me about that."

"Don't get me wrong," Sam said. "I love my dad. But wow, is he a mess."

Sam's father was an entrepreneur just like her. Throughout Sam's childhood, he was always quitting jobs or getting laid off. Then he'd start a business. The business would fail. And he'd go back to working for someone else or start another business. The last company he founded was successful. But he made a series of bad business decisions, ruined his relationship with his cofounders, and was eventually asked to leave. He ended up in corporate America "pushing pencils," according to Sam for the next 20 years until he retired. It was a future that Sam was doing everything in her power to avoid.

"It's just sad," Sam told me as she shook her head and let out another deep sigh. "He had so much potential. I'm going to screw up my business just like he did," she said in resignation. "I know it. I always do."

Sam was forecasting her future for me. But rather than writing an adventure tale where she was the hero—she was imagining a *horror story* where she was a powerless victim along for the ride.

We all have scary stories lurking in the shadows or beneath the surface that have the potential to slow us down, derail us, or stop us dead in our tracks. *They'll never go for it. It'll never work. I can't do it. What if…?* Those are all horror stories. When they're not managed, horror stories become so much a part of us that they seep into and permeate the fabric of our being. *I'm a failure. Our team is dysfunctional.*

These stories eventually write themselves. At their strongest, they become self-fulfilling prophecies. *Of course they hated it. I knew this would happen.* This is what was happening to Sam. And for the leaders and teams I work with, horror stories are one of the most powerful things that get in the way of them realizing their dreams. The problem with horror stories is that the more we focus on them, the more energy we spend on what we don't want to happen rather than what we do want to happen.

When I was younger, I was a terrible tennis player. I would focus so hard on where I *didn't* want the ball to go that I would inevitably hit it exactly there. Within millimeters. Every. Single. Time. Our mind's ability to focus on possible futures—desirable or not—determines what our bodies do unconsciously. Once I learned to focus on where I wanted the ball to go rather than where I didn't want it to go, I began to hit the ball into the right place on the tennis court.

In *The Inner Game of Tennis*, former tennis instructor, Tim Gallwey, talks about what is now common practice in sports psychology, as well as its cousin, leadership coaching: visualize your desired future and let that vision guide you. Over time, the more your vision becomes a part of how you think, the desired behavior becomes part of your muscle memory, and the less you need to think about it.[1]

While horror stories arise from our innate need to survive, they overtake our ability to have visions that can help us thrive. Or if we have the vision, the horror stories overtake our ability to accomplish our mission or act as miserable speed bumps along the way. It's like Sam was leading her life the way I used to play tennis. She spent so much energy focusing on what she didn't want to happen, that she unwittingly made a lot of it happen.

"I'm probably blowing this way out of proportion," Sam countered right after she admitted her deepest and darkest fear. "I mean, I know I'm not my dad…" "And I love my dad, don't get me wrong. I'm such a jerk."

Sam continued: "I can't believe I'm talking about him in this way. I can't believe I'm talking about myself in this way. I think I need to be more positive. People tell me that all the time. Things are good, right? We just raised a Series B! Not a lot of women do that. I should be thankful…"

Conventional wisdom is no match for our deepest and darkest fears.

In Western culture, we talk about things like facing and conquering our fears as strengths and virtues. And we generally value positivity and optimism. Combine them when things are terrifying, and a lot of us feel

---

1. W. Timothy Gallwey, *The Inner Game of Tennis: The Classic Guide to the Mental Side of Peak Performance*, rev. ed. (New York: Random House, Trade Paperbacks, 2008).

like we must either diminish how bad or scary things are or fight the fears by compartmentalizing or reframing them.

Fighting your horror stories is like fighting your internal kryptonite—you can try to do it, but you'll probably lose. Because as ugly and undesirable as they are, they're a part of you. Or if you win, they'll eventually return. That's how horror stories work.

The technical term for this is a *false ending*. The best horror stories have them at the end—sometimes a few of them. But there are also times when your ability to confabulate horrific possible futures is actually a superpower, as my grandmother learned in 1939. Like waking nightmares, our horror stories are alerting us that something is wrong.

Rather than fight them, you're better off honoring them. Only then will you know what to do with them.

Embracing Your Horror Stories

In the *Buffy The Vampire Slayer* episode "Nightmares," a demon with the ability to make your worst fears come true invades Sunnyvale, the fictional town where Buffy lives. One by one, Buffy and each of her friends must face their fears. Sometimes, they can slay what scares them—demons, vampires, and other frightening things. Other times, they can avoid what scares them—tarantulas, for example—by simply running away. And for some fears—feeling like you're not enough or that you're too much, for example—the only way to manage the fears is to find out if they are true. If they are true, they can exist. If not, they disappear. Luckily for Buffy and her gang, the fears are not true. In real life, however, managing your fears is a little more nuanced than that. But it's just as straightforward.

This ability to see the worst is what we call *pessimism*. It's not pretty. And it's something that a lot of us spend a lot of energy fighting. Like all superpowers, overusing this has a terrible cost. But underusing it has a similar cost. We see this in Neil Gaiman's Sandman.

In the comic book and television adaptation, Dream—aka Sandman—is an all-powerful being who has the ability to create dreams and nightmares. When he loses this ability, humanity enters into a long period of sleeping sickness, an illness that causes fatigue, insomnia, and comas. Humanity needs the Sandman—and his dreams and nightmares—to learn, grow, and function. This is the case in real life, as well. We need our nightmares as much as we need our dreams. There just has to be a balance.

The ability to prognosticate scary futures in just the right amount is what psychologists call *defensive pessimism*. It's essentially pessimism with a purpose. It was this ability that helped my grandmother see what others couldn't see, called her to action, and ultimately helped her survive. It's an ability that the most successful leaders I work with have—in the right amount. And it's one that you can develop. According to psychologists Todd Kashdan and Robert Biswas-Diener:

> *Rather than firmly holding a perpetually sunny outlook and avoiding negative thoughts and feelings, defensive pessimists allow themselves to imagine how they will feel if things turn out badly…By imagining worst-case scenarios, defensive pessimists can transform their anxiety into action, implementing plans that can mitigate disaster.*[2]

Strategic planning meetings are one way to embrace this ability. But when your fears feel personal—to you or your team—you need to face them in a different way. To move forward, Sam needed to explore her horror stories on her own first. Exploring them with Dara only ended in him calling her a pessimist and them fighting. She needed to give these stories room to breathe in order to figure out what to do with them.

---

2. Todd B. Kashdan, Ph.D. and Robert Biswas-Diener, *The Upside of Your Dark Side: Why Being Your Whole Self—Not Just Your "Good" Self—Drives Success and Fulfillment* (New York: Penguin Random House, 2015).

"That's a good story," I said to Sam with a smile during one of her cyclical pauses as she forecasted her future and then criticized herself for being so negative.

"Huh? What story?"

"The story about you turning into your father," I clarified. "It's Kafkaesque." I was referring to one of the most terrifying change narratives ever written, *The Metamorphosis*, by Franz Kafka. In this story, a man named Gregor Samsa awakes one morning to find himself transformed into a gigantic cockroach.

The best stories are about transformation, which is the journey that Sam was on as she transformed from a brilliant web developer into an entrepreneur and CEO. Heroes change themselves, and they change the world. Yet, as exciting as the prospect of change is for many people, it's equally as terrifying. This story is a terrifying example of what it feels like not to be in control of your transformation or life. It's a feeling that a lot of the founders and executives I work with feel at the beginning, middle, and throughout their journey.

"Ugh, you're right. Here I go again… I really need to stop being so negative. Most of this is probably not true, anyway."

"Let's play," I offered.

Once I explained the benefit of defensive pessimism, Sam stopped fidgeting and perked up. Her limbic system calmed down as she got curious and got out of a fight-or-flight mode. For the first time since we started talking, she looked me in the eyes.

"OK, I'll try," she said.

I invited Sam to take a few minutes to imagine all the things that could go wrong as she grew her company and to list them all out.

"We're going for quantity, not quality," I told her. These stories could be real, fantasy, whatever. "Are you familiar with the Double Diamond?" I asked referring to a design model popular in the tech world.

"I think?" Sam said. She had worked in tech for a long time, but there was so much jargon to sort through and everyone had their own definitions of how things should work.

"We're at the beginning of the first diamond. We're going big, exploring all the possibilities. We're not committing to anything. Go deep, go dark. This is a creative exercise."

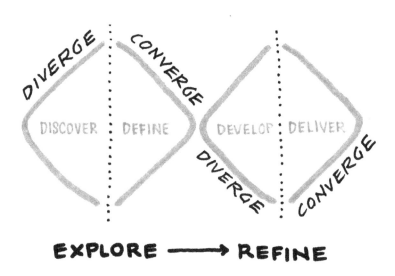

In the tech world, and in the practice of design thinking more broadly, we often use divergent and convergent thinking when coming up with ideas. Sometimes, we visualize this way of working as two double diamonds.[3] The beginning of the two diamonds requires divergent thinking—going big and broad with a problem—and the end of the diamonds requires convergent thinking as we converge on a problem definition and then a solution.

---

3. Jonathan Ball, "The Double Diamond: A Universally Accepted Depiction of the Design Process," Design Council, www.designcouncil.org.uk/news-opinion/double-diamond-universally-accepted-depiction-design-process

And sometimes, we think of the messy first stage as exploring branching opportunities and the second as refining our ideas, as Bill Buxton illustrates in his classic *Sketching User Experiences*.[4] Entertaining your horror stories requires the same stance: explore and then refine.

When doing this for your horror stories, it's most fun and fruitful if you add a literary twist. Fiction writer, Stephen King, likes to use the What if? question to come up with his scariest horror stories, which are replete with heroes and villains alike. For example, the question, "What if vampires invaded a small New England village?" led to the 1975 bestseller, *Salem's Lot*. It is a simple question with a delightfully engaging 672-page answer.[5] Entertaining your what-ifs in a safe space will uncover the worst possible futures you can imagine so that you can objectively assess the validity and severity of your fears. Doing so will help you see when your fears are or are not founded, while helping you minimize risk.

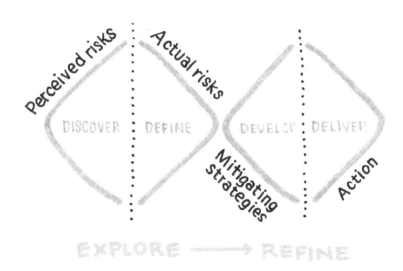

4. Bill Buxton, *Sketching User Experiences: Getting the Design Right and the Right Design* (San Francisco, CA: Morgan Kaufmann, 2007).
5. Stephen King, *On Writing: A Memoir of the Craft* (New York: Scribner, 2000).

As Sam identified her horror stories, she came up with a long list of things that scared her. As she broke down her stories, she made them more tangible than the amorphic, "I'm going to turn into my dad's story." Here was her list:

If things keep going this way, I'll:

- Never raise another round of funding.
- Disappoint my investors.
- Drive my cofounder to quit.
- Be pushed out of my company.
- Have to get a full-time job.
- Be miserable forever.
- Never be able to afford to buy a house.
- Always worry about money.
- Be stressed, anxious, and unhappy.
- Realize this will all have been pointless and that I should have stopped while I was ahead.

As Sam forecasted her future, she got more and more sullen. It was a lot to absorb.

"What's coming up for you right now?" I asked her as she brought this all to the surface.

"I'm scared," she said. "Petrified."

This is how horror stories work. They can be big and impede you from realizing your big-picture vision. Or they can be small and surface as you map your mission or after you head out on your journey. Either way, they can bring you to a stop.

At this point, I asked Sam to prioritize her list according to which stories were the scariest and potentially riskiest. When you identify impediments early on rather than pretending they don't exist, you can mitigate your risks and move forward much more effectively. Plus, it makes your story that much better.

As we went down Sam's list together, we saw that some stories were scary, and some were not so bad. The fear that she would disappoint her investors terrified her, for example. But when she imagined a future where that was real, she realized that it wasn't the end of the world. Sure, she would feel sad and disappointed. But she could work through those feelings.

Driving her cofounder out of the company, on the other hand, was not OK. She and Dara were good friends. She did not want to risk losing him, nor did she want to run the company without him. That was an important story that went to the top of her three scariest stories list, along with never being able to afford a house and having to get a full-time job.

"What comes up for you when you think about these three stories?" I asked.

"I'm terrified," Sam answered. "If the top one comes true, I don't want to run my company anymore. If the second comes true, I will resent the fact that I spent all these years as an entrepreneur, not making enough money to live the life that I want. And if I fail and am forced to get a job, I'll be devastated. I don't want any of them to happen."

The thing about stories, however, is that when your brain can't tell the difference between the stories you hear, experience, or imagine, they may as well be true. And when they feel true, they determine our actions—actions that may be useful or, more likely, work against us meeting our goals and fulfilling our mission.

Starting with her top scariest story, Sam and I unpacked its validity.

"If things keep going this way, I'll drive my cofounder to quit," I said. "Is that true?"

"Yes," Sam answered confidently.

"How do you know?" I asked, genuinely curious.

"Well, Dara has said so on more than one occasion."

"What is it about the way things are going that needs to change according to Dara?"

"He wants me to stop micromanaging his engineers and running the product team in circles with changing feature sets week to week."

"It sounds like this is a blocker," I offered, using language that Sam was used to. In tech, serious bugs or issues that impede a product from going to market or customers from using the product are *blockers*. As such, they must be removed and become a top priority to fix. Anything else is a *nice to have.*

"Yeah…it's funny," she responded. "Working on my management style is one of the things I want to work on with you. But it honestly never felt like a priority. I figured it would be the bottom of our list while I worked on more important things."

"Like what?"

"I don't know," she said. "I'm always putting out fires. My priorities change day to day, week to week. I'm so busy keeping the business afloat that I never have the headspace to think about soft skills like that. Yet now it seems like something I have to figure out or this whole thing can't work. But you're right. It is a blocker."

"This is your story," I reminded Sam with a smile. "I'm just repeating what I hear."

"Yeah…" she said with a deep sigh. "OK. What do I do about this?"

"Let's first dig into your top three. I think you'll know what to do next after that. Tell me about not being able to buy a home."

As Sam dug into her nightmares, it was clear what she had to do. If things continued as they were going, she would not be able to save up a down payment to buy a home. This felt like another blocker for her. As much as she dreamed of running her own business, she also dreamed of owning a home. After her father was pushed out of his business when she was a child, her family had to sell their home and rent. She saw how hard it was for her parents to deal with rent increases, negligent land-lords, and having to move when the cost of living in their neighborhood got too expensive. She wanted to know what it felt like to experience owning her own home. It motivated and excited her.

When she wasn't working, Sam watched home renovation shows on TV and dreamed about what she would do if she could renovate her own home. To do this, however, Sam had to reimagine her business's core revenue model. They had to make more money, or this whole thing wouldn't work—and she wouldn't turn her dream of owning a home into reality.

"That's easy!" Sam exclaimed once she realized that this was all she had to do. "I know exactly who to call." While rethinking revenue models isn't necessarily easy, Sam's next steps were easy: bring in a financial analyst and start experimenting with new revenue models or whatever they recommended. She was sure this could be done—she'd seen it hap-pen at a few other startups she had worked with over the years. If they couldn't figure it out, then she would have a serious issue on her hands. But what felt like a horror story before now felt like a mystery for her and Dara to solve. It went from a problem to a puzzle. Sam loved solv-ing puzzles as much as she loved mysteries.

"Ooh…" she said as she tapped her fingertips together like someone who is scheming something exciting. "This is going to be fun."

For her third scariest story—failing and having to find a full-time job—when we unpacked this one, we realized that it was true. If her business failed, she would have to find a full-time job. She did not want to risk digging into the savings she had set aside to buy her future home.

"How do you feel about that?" I asked. "If this doesn't work out, you'll have to get a job."

Sam paused for a minute and took a few deep breaths. "I'll live," she said. "I'll be devastated, don't get me wrong. I'll be devastated, but I'll live. And then I'll save up enough or find the right investors and do it all over again. Or maybe I'll consult for a while. I know lots of founders who do that in between companies as they recoup their energy. I hadn't thought of that. Of course. Hmm…" she said as she sat firmly upright in her chair. "I can do this."

After letting Sam soak this in for a moment, now it was my turn to ask her what she wanted to do with what she now knew.

We left that day with a clear plan of action for Sam, as well as her company. Her top priority over the next quarter was to work on her management skills. This would free her up to work on the next priority, which was her company vision—something that the investors and Dara were begging her to focus on. At the same time, she would call her financial consultant to see if they could help rethink their revenue model and work on some forecasting. Within six months, she wanted to have re-earned the confidence of Dara, her investors, and her team. She wanted to see revenue ticking upward. And she wanted to feel good about continuing to dream about her future home.

With a vision, a mission, and a plan, Sam was ready to make things happen. Ultimately, she reauthored her horror stories. But she didn't do that by denying their existence or letting them subconsciously control her actions. She appreciated them, thanked them for their service, and used them to move forward. Only then was she able to recoup the energy and excitement she needed to do her job. She would need it—because her job was not easy. But for the first time in a long time, it felt like something she could do.

Over time, she learned to stop micromanaging and changing priorities daily. To do so, she instead focused on guiding her company with a clear vision and growth model that people could get excited by. As a result, her relationship with Dara is stronger, revenue is up, engagement is up, and attrition is down. She lets down her investors from time to time and, as suspected, can roll with it—the company is doing well enough that she can handle things not being perfect all of the time. She still hasn't bought that home, but has enough money saved to either move to a cheaper city and buy something or spend a few more years saving. That's an adventure she's much more excited by than the horror stories she used to entertain.

If you find yourself paralyzed by fear or fighting yourself, search in the shadows or beneath the surface for hidden horror stories that might be holding you back. Anything big that you want to accomplish—starting a team, creating a new product, founding a company, selling a company, or taking on investors—can be scary. When things are scary, we tell ourselves stories to keep us safe. Sometimes those stories are true. Sometimes they're not.

If you find yourself confabulating terrifying possible futures that impede you from accomplishing your mission, don't look away. First, give yourself a pat on the back. Or possibly a hug—you might need it. Your brain is functioning exactly as it should. It's protecting you.

Next, appreciate what scares you. There might be some real threats lurking in the shadows. And there might not. Then figure out what you do and don't need to actually worry about or plan for and adapt your mission accordingly. Fighting it or trying to compartmentalize your fears won't work. And it's a waste of energy. You'll need that energy to do your actual job: leading others forward.

TRY THIS

As you look at the journey ahead of you, what scares you the most? On the left side of a piece of paper, list all your fears, risks, and assumptions that may or may not be true. For each item, identity whether it is true, false, or unknown. What is the riskiest assumption you're making that if you don't test soon can get you into trouble? Prioritize your list accordingly. On the right side, write what you can do to prevent, circumvent, or face the highest priority items on your list. From that, pull out your highest priority action items that will help you accomplish your mission and reach your goals.

IV

Impact

We do not have to become heroes overnight. Just one step at a time, meeting each thing that comes up, seeing it is not as dreadful as it appeared, discovering we have the strength to stare it down.

—Eleanor Roosevelt

8

Assessing Your Impact

Nichelle Nichols, who played Lieutenant Uhura in the original *Star Trek*, was one of the first Black women to have a leading role on an American network television. After the first season ended in 1967, however, Nichols was ready to quit. She faced racism—subtle and not so subtle—at the television studio. For example, after fellow cast member, Grace Lee, was released from the show, the assistant of a senior executive told Nichols, "If anyone was let go, it should have been you, not Grace Lee. Ten of you could never equal one blue-eyed blonde." Later, she was told by a couple of mailroom employees that they had been ordered not to give her the bags of fan mail she had been receiving. "This was the ultimate humiliation," she recounted in her autobiography.[1]

So, she gave Gene Roddenberry, *Star Trek's* creator, her resignation.

"You can't," Roddenberry told her. "You don't see what I'm trying to achieve." He asked her to think about it over the weekend.

But Nichols had just been offered the role of her dreams. She was a stage actor and dancer. She wanted to be on Broadway, not wearing costumes and jaunting around the universe with aliens on TV. She was on a mission—her mission, not Roddenberry's. Her mind was set.

That weekend, Nichols was a celebrity guest at an NAACP fundraiser in Beverly Hills. The organizer wanted to introduce Nichols to one of her biggest fans. To her surprise, that fan turned out to be Dr. Martin Luther King, Jr. He walked across the room to Nichols and told her, "I am your greatest fan."

Nichols was honored. She thanked Dr. King, and then she proudly told him about her impending departure and plans for the future.

"You cannot do that," Dr. King replied. "Don't you understand what [Gene Roddenberry] has achieved?"

Incredulous, she let him continue. He was "my leader," she recalled in a 2010 interview with Archive of American Television, speaking of Dr. King.[2]

"For the first time, we are being seen the world over as we should be seen," he continued. "Do you understand that this is the only show my wife Coretta and I will allow our little children to stay up and watch?"[3]

1. Nichelle Nichols, *Beyond Uhura: Star Trek and Other Memories* (New York: G.P. Putnam, 1994).
2. https://interviews.televisionacademy.com/interviews/nichelle-nichols?clip=112689#interview-clips
3. "*Star Trek*'s Uhura Reflects on MLK Encounter," NPR, January 17, 2011, www.npr.org/2011/01/17/132942461/Star-Treks-Uhura-Reflects-On-MLK-Encounter

Nichols clearly did not understand. She wasn't receiving her fan mail. She was working too much to watch *Star Trek* on TV.

Nichols knew who she was, what her superpowers were, and what mission she was on—she was a politically engaged dancer and stage actor who blazed trails as a Black woman all the way to Broadway. She also understood her kryptonite—the racism she encountered every day on set.

She was clear about her story. But she was not yet clear on the full story.

Until she was.

Each week, Nichols beamed into American homes, demonstrating that a Black woman could and should participate in and was integral to a civil society of the future. She embodied and lived her and Dr. King's collective dream—Gene Roddenberry's dream, too. She didn't need to change her course to make an impact. She was making an impact. Instead, she had to fully see and appreciate the story she was already living.

Nichols withdrew her resignation.

I'm glad she did. Twenty-five years later, *Star Trek* was broadcast into my home and Nichols showed me that a woman could use computers, be totally badass while doing so, and boldly go…anywhere. She did the same for many of the amazing women I have had the honor of working with throughout my career.

The world is a better place because of this.

When you're busy leading others, you can't always see the impact that you have and can have—your full who, what, and why—your 360 story. You see your version, but that's just one part of a much bigger picture. When you're a leader, your story is not solely your own. It's who you are, what you do, and also the difference you make in the world. The clearer you are on your impact, the more effectively you will amplify your impact.

Uncovering Your Full Story

A few years ago, I was working with Javier, the founder and CEO of a rapidly scaling startup. His company was doubling in size year-to-year, which was thrilling. But he struggled to scale his leadership to keep up with that fast pace. As a founder, he had many strengths that enabled him to start, build, and grow his company. But there was something standing in his way: Javier was a terrible listener. No matter how much he tried, he could not figure out how to reauthor this story. This was the number one complaint he heard from his team, his board, his partner, his family—everyone.

While his board tried to work around him, this approach could last for only so long. He was waiting for them to give him an ultimatum: learn to be a better leader or get out of the way. The more he stressed about this, the more impatient and dismissive he became. It was a terrible cycle. And it was a big problem.

Javier's inability to listen drove his executive team nuts—he was seen by others as brash and dismissive. It's a common myth or fantasy that this is the kind of personality that makes for a great founder. While a lot of founders share these characteristics in the early days of their company, they usually start to backfire at some point.

When you work with enough Javiers, like I do, you see this a lot: their inability to listen to others starts to impede business growth, innovation, and speed to market when it matters most. And it decreases morale, engagement, and problem solving among the people they interact with—executives and individual contributors alike. All of this affects people. And it ultimately affects the bottom line.

When we looked at Javier's past, his inability to listen stuck out like a big red flag. Throughout his life, it was not anything that he was able to get over. As much as he tried, he kept running into the same issues and getting the same feedback—unofficially and officially in those dreaded employee performance surveys that he asked his chief operating officer to implement a year earlier when performance started to suffer.

The limitation of mining from your past is that you can only see what you see. You can't see what others see. It's an important place to start, but it's not enough. And the limitation of most employee performance surveys is that they focus on what's broken rather than showing you how to amplify what's working.

"Can you help me be a better listener?" Javier asked me the first time we met. His key investor and mentor, Julia, begged him to see me so that he could stop getting in his company's way and start acting like a CEO. Javier was determined to figure this out. "It's my biggest problem," he continued. "Maybe there's a book I should read? Or homework you can give me? I just can't figure it out."

"What have you tried so far?" I asked.

"You name it! Active listening, books, videos, mindfulness, meditation. I've tried it all."

"I can see that you really want to make this work."

"I'm desperate."

By the time they come to me for help, people like Javier usually are at their wit's end. "Can you help me?"

"Sure, we can work on your listening skills. But you're probably not going to listen to anything I tell you," I continued with a smile.

Javier sat back, crossed his arms, let out a long sigh, and then laughed. "OK, you got me."

"Have you heard of the paradoxical theory of change?" Javier had done his undergraduate studies in psychology, so I figured I'd ask.

"I haven't heard that one. Tell me more."

The *paradoxical theory of change* is a term coined by psychiatrist Arnold Beisser in 1970. According to Beisser, as much as we want to change ourselves or other people, it's hard to change who and how we are. Change is risky, scary, and hard. But we often need to change. If you want to change, rather than fight yourself, you're much better off becoming fully aware of who you are and how you operate. Once you do, you can use that insight and awareness to move forward.[4]

"You're smart," I told Javier. "I have no doubt that you can learn a new skill like this. But if you're fighting yourself this hard and enlist me to tell you what to do, you'll just fight me, too. We'll end up right where we started a few months from now wondering what went wrong."

I had seen this occur enough times to speak confidently from experience.

"I don't want to waste your time or my time. I know you don't want to, either."

Javier let out another deep sigh as he sat up straight and re-crossed his arms. "OK, what do we do?"

Javier and I devised a plan to uncover his full story—not just the story that he told me or the story that people wrote in their feedback reports. We would find out how people experienced working with him by asking them to tell us stories. My hunch was that these stories weren't always negative, or Javier wouldn't have been able to start his company and grow it as successfully as he did. Once we had enough stories, we would combine them all into a coherent narrative. To do that, we needed to enlist other people and collaborate with them. Something had to be working. But at this point, Javier's vision was so clouded by what was going wrong that he couldn't see what had gone right.

We started by identifying the people who mattered most to him and the success of his business—his support system. We would start with his executive team and then talk to his most difficult board member, a

---

4. Arnold Beisser, "The Paradoxical Theory of Change," in *Gestalt Therapy Now*, ed. Joen Fagan and Irma Lee Shepherd (New York: Harper & Row, 1970), 77–80.

challenging investor, the cofounder from his previous company, and his boyfriend, James, who knew Javier better than anyone. I would interview them to find out what was working about Javier's leadership and how he showed up in the world and what could be even better.

Next, we outlined what we wanted to learn, and we agreed on who would do the interviews. You uncover a much more complete story when you interview people rather than asking them to fill out a form or write a letter. It worked when I made documentary films and when I helped tech companies uncover customer insights. And I experienced it for myself when my coach uncovered my own 360 story for me as I pivoted my business years ago. If for some reason you can't interview people, written evaluations and surveys are the next best thing. But if you can talk to people, do it.

After I met with everyone, Javier and I agreed that we would debrief, deconstruct, and synthesize what we learned together. We would take the good, the bad, and the ugly and see what story emerged. Once we had a better understanding of what his story was and could be, we would figure out a plan for what to do next—we'd either set out to make the story better, amplify it, or both.

"What do you think?" I asked Javier after we came up with this plan.

"Honestly, I'm nervous."

"Yeah, it requires a lot of vulnerability to put yourself out there like this."

"No, no, no. It's not that," he clarified. "This is going to take a few weeks. That's time that we could better spend training me to be a better listener, no?"

The biggest challenge with a project like this is that even if another person does it for you, it takes time. Javier was anxious about making progress sooner rather than later, so we agreed to work on his listening skills together while I spent a few weeks conducting my interviews. This way, he could be sure that he wasn't missing anything important when he tried to teach himself how to listen from books and videos.

Javier was a data person and wanted to know that he had tried everything before changing course.

Over the next few weeks, Javier and I worked on his skills. It turns out that he already knew much of what I taught him about how to be a good listener. He had spent weeks reading articles and watching online videos on the topic before seeking my help. But he struggled to put it into action. Knowing *how* to listen was not the issue. Something else was in the way. But at least he could cross "learn listening skills" off his to-do list. Knowing how to listen was not his problem.

Finding your 360 story works a lot like finding your identity narrative by mining your past experiences. The biggest difference is that you are getting out of your head and mining your system to understand how people experience working with you as a leader. When you combine them all, you'll have a better view of your full story.

This is important—every leader works within and needs to impact their work system. Otherwise, you're just a lone wolf. Marvel hero, Wolverine spent years on his own before joining the X-Men. Lone wolves can be superheroes, sure. But they're much more powerful when they're part of a team.

To find your 360 story, you want to answer similar questions as you do when you mine your past. While every context is different, and you will have your own areas you'd like to cover, the story should cover the following points:

- What you are trying to achieve?
- What do you do that's effective?
- How can you become even more effective?
- What impact do you have—on other people, on your business, on the world—that's tangible, measurable, and emotional?
- How can you have an even greater impact?

Combine all that and you've got a decent story to work with.

Two Different Javiers

When Javier and I met to debrief his story, he was apprehensive.

"They hate me, don't they?" he asked with a coy smile. "Lay it on me, Doc."

What I learned in those interviews, and what Javier learned in our debrief, surprised us both. Despite people complaining to him for years that he was a terrible listener, when he was at his best, he was actually a very good listener. It's how he attracted a world-class executive team, how he raised his first and second rounds of funding, and how he engaged his customers and built products that they loved.

He listened. And when he listened, he listened *deeply*.

Unbeknownst to him, it was one of his superpowers. At least it was according to his system.

"What?!" Javier exclaimed as we unpacked my transcripts. He was as delighted and confused as was I.

"Does that sound familiar to you?"

"Not at all," he beamed. He loved defying expectations. As much as this confused him, it also delighted him.

"OK, let's continue to dig into the data."

As we knew, there were times when Javier didn't listen. When, for example, a junior-level designer pitched a product idea or demoed a new feature, Javier was a terrible listener. When an executive or board member came to him with a serious concern, he was terrible. It was a mystery. And it was not a mystery that his people system could figure out for him. Javier had to figure it out for himself.

"I'm seeing two different Javiers," I said. "The one who listens deeply. And the one who doesn't listen. What creates that difference?"

"I remember that particular pitch!" Javier said as he almost jumped up from his chair, referring to one of the examples that came out of our interviews. "It was terrible!"

"What about it was terrible?"

"I don't know. I remember feeling extremely anxious in that meeting. I think I was very mean to that designer. I do remember that. I felt bad, but it was terrible."

As we unpacked this further, Javier and I learned that he listened best when he trusted the other person. He felt safest when he did not feel like he was going to be criticized or called out as the fraud that he often thought he was. (Impostor syndrome affects more successful people than you could imagine.)

"What tells you that you can feel safe and trust someone when they come to you with an idea?" I asked him. I knew he could trust people.

His highest performing executives told me that they knew that he trusted them implicitly. It was one of the things they appreciated most about him.

"Hmmm . . . They let me know that they've considered all the options before they come to me with an idea. Then I know that I can trust them."

"Did this designer consider all their options before they pitched their idea?"

"Hell, no. At least I don't think so? I guess I don't know…" he said as he trailed off and slumped back into his chair.

As we unpacked his story even further, I learned that Javier grew up in a family with a mercurial, impatient father who was a terrible listener and who spoke before he thought. His father meant well, but Javier felt awful being on the receiving end of his father's criticism. And there was a lot of it. The only way Javier and his sisters knew how to manage this behavior was to mirror their father's behavior: not listen to him, think as little as possible, and talk right back—loudly and quickly.

It worked. This ability to not listen was an asset in the Medina family. It was something the family was really good at, and it became the family's story. It was an asset in Javier's early days as a trailblazing marketing manager known for bucking industry trends and creating his own way of doing things. But as a CEO, it was now holding him back.

"So, you listen when you trust that people have done their due diligence?"

"Yeah…" Javier said. "Hmm…" he muttered as he put his hand to his face, looked off into the distance, and started thinking.

"Is it really that easy?" he asked after a minute.

"Is what that easy?"

"Can I just ask people to do their due diligence before pitching me? Or before anything? Meetings, emails, conversations, workshops? It's infuriating when people don't do their homework. Why can't they just do their homework! It would all be so much easier if they could do their homework before we meet…" Javier said.

At this point, Javier and I had been working together for long enough that he could already preempt my next question and answer it. Why not? There was no reason why not. It was worth a try.

Javier and I spent the next six months experimenting with different ways to get people to do their homework before meeting with him. As suspected, he was an excellent listener at those times. The more he listened, the more people trusted him and vice versa. And the more they trusted one another, the better he, his executive team, and individual contributors around the company worked together. The better they worked together, the faster they innovated, met deadlines, and brought new features to market.

And for the times when Javier couldn't request that people do their due diligence before they met, he figured out another way. When, for example, he got frustrated in board meetings, he learned to pause, take a deep breath, and remember that he was probably missing key data. Once he calmed down, he learned to engage with board members by asking genuine, open questions rather than accusing them of doing something sinister, which was part of his previous modus operandi. It took a lot of trial and error, but Javier eventually mastered this new way of working.

Eventually, this story that he was a good listener became the story that he and everyone he worked with experienced over and over again. The more they experienced it, the more effective he and everyone he worked with were at their jobs, and the more successful his business was. This story became a part of Javier and his organization and how they operated. The reason for this was part neuroscience, part organizational psychology.

Paving Pathways

When you experience stories—real, told, heard, lived, and projected—they don't only become a part of how you think and operate. They imprint themselves onto your brain's neural pathways. They physically become part of you. The more you experience your stories, the stronger these stories get. The stronger they get, the more real they feel. They function like a habit over time—they're just how you operate without having to think.[5] You're convinced you're too quiet, you get quieter. You know that you're a good listener, you are a good listener.

If you uncover a new narrative and want to overwrite your previous narrative, the secret is not to *say* it over and over again—you must *live* it over and over again. In doing so, you will pave new neural pathways with your new story as the old pathways fade away.

This is how stories ultimately work. Stories are not just something we tell other people—they're something that you absorb into your physical being. Your stories make up who you are as a person in the abstract. And they are a part of your brain. You are your stories. Literally.

Organizations work in much the same way. Only instead of neural pathways, they have physical hallways and virtual corridors that are paved via connections between humans over landlines and airwaves. Stories—your stories, other people's stories, collective stories—pave themselves onto these pathways and become a part of how your work system operates. Over time, the stories not only become real, but they also become inextricably intertwined in how your system works.[6] If you want to change

5. Lewis Mehl-Madrona, M.D., Ph.D. with Barbara Mainguy, M.A., *Remapping Your Mind: The Neuroscience of Self-Transformation Through Story* (Rochester, VT: Bear & Company, 2015).
6. Markus Russin and Karin Thier, *Storytelling in Organizations: A Narrative Approach to Change, Brand, Project and Knowledge Management* (Heidelberg: Springer Berlin, 2018).

your system, you must change your stories. To change your stories, you must change yourself. To effectively change yourself and sustain this transformation, you must involve your system. In doing so, you will also transform your system, which is part of your job as a leader.

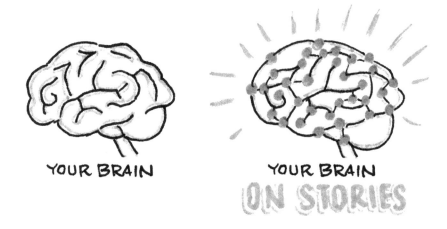

YOUR BRAIN

YOUR BRAIN
ON STORIES

9

Managing Conflict

When my son, Max, was 2 years old, he was obsessed with our dog, Ralph. Ralph is a scrappy little terrier mutt who does not like kids. As much as Max wanted to be friends with Ralph, he was also afraid of him—the dog sometimes snapped at him—so Max quickly learned to keep his distance. Or if he did engage, the interaction would usually end in tears.

That Halloween, Max dressed up like a superhero—putting on his cape and doing his favorite superhero moves. As excited as he was for his first time to be trick-or-treating as a sentient toddler, something wasn't right. Max seemed despondent, like he was missing something—like a superhero without a cape.

He looked at me earnestly and said, "Mom, I think Ralph wants to be super too." He grabbed a dog treat, picked up Ralph's red puffy jacket that looks a lot like a cape when he wears it, and yelled across the room, "Hey, Ralph, let's be super together!"

Ralph came for the treat, sat down next to Max, and gave him a high five (sitting and giving high fives are two of the three tricks Ralph will do for treats). Then they posed together like true superheroes. No biting, no tears. Just two superfriends being super together.

What Max learned that day was what it takes a lot of us years to figure out.

First, superheroes don't exist in a vacuum and never work alone. Batman and Robin, Justice League, X-Men, Buffy and her gang—superheroes are more super when they partner with and lead others to greatness.

Second, to be most super, owning your own story as a leader is not enough—you also need to help others find their stories, thereby turning them into superheroes.

It's not easy to partner with or lead others. It can be scary and feel dangerous. But when you're on a mission, you need to figure out how to do it. This will not only make you feel more super, but it will also amplify your impact and make your whole story that much better.

Conflict on the Executive Team

When I started working with Akshay, the founder of a health-tech company, he was facing a similar problem to Max's, but he didn't realize it. He had recently raised a successful round of funding that would help him grow while exponentially increasing the impact of his business. His mandate was clear: to revolutionize patient healthcare—not just for those privileged enough to afford it, but for the world at large. He was passionate. He was motivated. He was on a mission. He knew this wouldn't be easy. But he was excited and energized by the challenge ahead.

When Akshay first approached me about working together, however, he was despondent. "Why don't people listen to me?" he asked. He looked and sounded like a sad puppy, not someone who had recently raised over a hundred million dollars from international investors.

"I tell them what to do. They say yes, and then…crickets. I ask them what they want to do, same. Or maybe they tell me that they're going to work on something and months later…nothing. They don't follow through."

Akshay was in the process of building a world-class executive team. He was as adept at recruiting as he was at raising funds. Whether he was pitching a deck in a board room, meeting for coffee, or on a call, he had an uncanny ability to connect with people, connect them to his vision, and enlist their help.

He expertly maintained this connection with his investors—they had systems of working together in which he thrived—scheduled board meetings, presentations, reports, routine calls. When he had time to prepare, he could engage them very well. But when he had to work every day with his executive team and growing teams across his company, he floundered.

"I don't understand," he continued. "It's not like I haven't managed people before."

While Akshay was a young, first-time founder, he had previously managed a high-profile team of engineers at one of the largest and most successful tech companies in the world. After that, he ran his own startup for a few years, where he successfully managed a core team of mostly engineers. His teams loved him. And he loved them. He was a superstar.

Now that his company was doubling in size every year, he had to rely on a core team of a handful of executives to get things done. They were not getting along.

When we unpacked what was going on, we uncovered a few stories lurking beneath the surface that were getting in his and everyone else's way. For one thing, Akshay was insecure about what kind of a leader he was. He was mild-mannered, thoughtful, and quiet—not brash, impulsive, and loud, which is what he thought people expected of him. Once we got clear on his real story—identity, superpowers, mission, and all— he started to feel confident about his ability to lead. He was already doing it. He just didn't realize it.

So why didn't his new team listen to him? What was getting in his way were the stories he told himself about *other* people. Like all stories, the more he focused on those stories, the more they became true. Akshay had to learn how to check his stories, collaborate with his team, and ultimately write a new story together—many stories over many years, if he played this right.

A World in Conflict

Imagine that you're driving in the middle lane of a three-lane highway on a bright, sunny day. You're cool as a cucumber. Happy to be alive. All is good in the world. Suddenly, a car driving much slower than you merges onto the highway and meanders into your lane. You wait for them to pick up speed. But no. The car continues along at a respectable pace slightly below the speed limit.

"What a jerk!" you think to yourself as your heart races, bringing your blood to a rolling boil. "How unsafe!" you think, even though the other driver is well within the limits of safe driving. Are you actually in danger? Not really. Frustrated, yes. But perfectly safe. Nonetheless, your brain reacts to the situation as if you were in grave danger.

Before you have time to think another thought, your heart starts pounding, your vision narrows, and your fists clench tightly onto the steering wheel. You check to make sure there are no cars to your left because you would never want to cut someone else off, lest you be as rude and careless as that other driver. You see a tight opening, and you swerve into the fast lane, so you can pass this jerk, get back into the safety and flow of your middle lane, and be back on your merry way. In doing so, you dangerously cut off another car, which is exactly what started this whole situation in the first place.

As you pass the original culprit, you briefly glance over to your right to see who could be so rude. You expect to see a trench coat–wearing, mustached driver cackling to himself, playing the caricature of a cartoon villain as you speed past.

But no.

You instead see a frail, diminutive, sweet-looking older man, slightly hunched over, hands clenched on the steering wheel at exactly 2 and 10 o'clock. He doesn't notice you because his eyes are on the road, exactly where they should be.

Oops.

You potentially put yourself and others in danger because of a story that wasn't true—a few stories, actually. As a resident of this planet, you will often find yourself in conflict with other people—whether they know it or not. This behavior is buried deep in your DNA.

It happens on the road. According to statistics compiled by the National Highway Traffic Safety Administration (NHTSA) and Auto Vantage, road rage incidents in the U.S. resulted in 12,610 injuries and 218 murders over a seven-year period.[1]

And it especially happens at work. Maybe you think that someone keeps trying to make you look bad in staff meetings, or a seemingly careless direct report habitually submits error-laden work late, causing you to miss deadlines and look bad. Whether the threat is real or perceived and you respond with passive aggression, gossip, anger, or avoidance, you will only make things worse. Your ultimate mission in life is to stay alive. When everyone's a lion, you react. Unfortunately, when you react in situations like this—whether it's on the highway or in the boardroom—you often escalate rather than resolve the situation. This is what was happening to both Akshay and his executive team, although they didn't realize it.

To understand how to remedy the situation, you first have to understand the underlying mechanics of what's happening when you are facing challenges with other humans, no matter how big, small, acute, or seemingly benign the issue might seem.

Whether you're on the savanna, on a highway, or at work, your brain can't tell the difference between a perceived threat and a real threat. You therefore react the same whether the threat is a saber-tooth tiger, someone driving slower than you on a highway, or someone saying the wrong thing to you in an important board meeting. As complex as humans are, we're also strangely simple when it comes to our reactions to stimuli. While trying to pet an unfriendly dog could be an actual

1. "Aggressive Driving and Road Rage," SafeMotorist, www.safemotorist.com/articles/road-rage/

physical threat, the type of threats you face at work in a typical knowledge industry will fall into a different category—that of perceived psychological threats.

When you're under threat, you confabulate stories that aren't very good and are likely to get you into trouble. But not just any stories. The stories you confabulate to make sense of other people's behavior are a special kind of fiction that turns innocent people into villains. "What a jerk!" for example. That's a story that may or may not be true. This is what psychologists call the *fundamental attribution error.*[2] Studies show that you are more likely to attribute someone's behavior to their character rather than to the situation that caused the behavior, whereas a situation is usually the real cause. You are essentially writing an identity narrative to explain someone's behavior.

"They never listen to me—they're so self-centered." "She said no to my project—she's so closed-minded." Those stories hold power over you. When you encounter a villain, you react. You do it so automatically that you don't even have to think about it. It's one of those features of being human. And it's also one of those pesky bugs.

It's easier to come to these kinds of conclusions than to take an extra step and think, "They're driving awfully slowly. I wonder what's going on?" Or, "I'm not sure they heard what I said because they're looking off into the distance and didn't respond to that last comment. I should check to see if they heard me. I really want to know what they think." Or, "She said no to my project without explaining why. I wonder why she said no—I should find out." In the modern world, while threat responses might feel productive, they are not. But we respond, nonetheless.

In the absence of data, we tell ourselves stories that may or may not be true—stories about ourselves, about what we can do, and especially about other people.

2. Lee Ross and Richard E. Nisbett, *The Person and the Situation: Perspectives of Social Psychology*, 2nd ed. (London: Pinter & Martin Ltd, 2011).

What happens next when you're in conflict with other people is part psychology, part neuroscience, and it sounds a lot like physics—Newton's third law of motion, specifically. For every action, there is an equal and opposite reaction. When you fight someone—even with words—they fight back. If you pull away, they pull away too. Psychologists call this *mirroring*. You experience this when you're watching a movie and your pulse quickens and palms get sweaty as a hero fights villains. In the same way, when you are a part of other people's stories, people react to you accordingly. The mirror neurons in their brains can't tell the difference between your actions, their experiences, and the stories they create to make sense of what's happening. If you fight or flee, other people have the same reaction to watching a TV show—their emotions, stories, and reactions respond in kind.

When someone does something to anger, disappoint, or rile you up, and you respond as if you're fighting or fleeing from a wild animal, you will amplify and extend the conflict rather than diffuse it. While you may think that the story is "what a jerk!" this story becomes your puppet master.

The antidote to this cycle is to break the cycle. In her 2016 Democratic National Convention speech, for example, Michelle Obama eloquently summed up how to do this. "When they go low," she said referring to sociopolitical challenges, "We go high." The problem is that it takes a lot of training, coaching, and practice to get to that point. For most of us, it does not come naturally. We are not wired to take the high road—especially when we feel under threat.

And when your stories own you, you're a jumble of neurons and reflexes. You're not a reasonable, reasoning human capable of effectively resolving whatever issue it is you're facing. The best way to effectively break the cycle is to regain your ability to think clearly, reason, and see the truth.

You need to rewrite the narrative. Luckily, for this kind of narrative, you don't need a speechwriter. But you do need to be curious, vulnerable, and open to collaboration.

Rewriting Your Narrative

When Akshay and I unpacked the stories that he was telling himself about other people, we found there were many stories in his way. One of the most problematic stories was one that involved his chief operating officer, a person whom he had just hired a few months earlier. They were not getting along.

"I think I made a huge mistake in hiring Lilia," he told me. "I tell her what I want her to do, and she doesn't listen to me. I tell her what I need, and she fights me every step of the way. She was a very expensive hire. She needs to go, right?" Things were so bad that he was convinced that he needed to fire her, which is what he initially asked me to help him with.

When we dug deeper, Akshay told me that Lilia was not dedicated to her job. More specifically, she spent too much time with her kids. "Look at this—kids, kids, kids. How, how can she do her job?" he asked me as he reviewed her shared online calendar in real time. "This is why she's not meeting her goals," he deduced. "I don't understand. She was so highly recommended."

"I don't think she's a hard enough worker," he said finally.

"That's a good story," I remarked as I told him about the fundamental attribution error and how we write identity narratives for people in times of stress. In reality, Akshay respected and admired Lilia. It's part of why he hired her in the first place. But something was kicking him into storytelling overdrive.

"Are you familiar with psychological safety?" I asked Akshay.

"Of course," he answered. "Silicon Valley is obsessed with the idea. It means that I have to coddle my employees to make them feel safe, right? It's so American…" he continued. "I'm half-kidding…I think?" he half-clarified bashfully as he grimaced with the embarrassment of someone who had just said too much.

In 2012, Google released their findings from a study called *Project Aristotle*. They set out to find out what the highest performing teams had in common. The highest factor on the list was psychological safety, "A belief that a team is safe for risk taking in the face of being seen as ignorant, incompetent, negative, or disruptive. In a team with high psychological safety, teammates feel safe to take risks around their team members. They feel confident that no one on the team will embarrass or punish anyone else for admitting a mistake, asking a question, or offering a new idea."[3]

I have heard many managers misinterpret these findings to mean "don't hurt people's feelings" over the years. This misinterpretation can't be farther from the truth. Teams with strong psychological safety have robust, healthy, productive conflict when they need to. They just don't act like feral animals, undermining their own efforts in the process. Teams that have their needs met are more engaged, more creative, and perform extremely well. They have full use of their brains and perform accordingly.

"This is less about coddling people and more about the science of how the brain works," I told Akshay as he perked up. He was a science guy. I'm a science gal. I was speaking his language.

According to neuroscience experts, David Rock and Christine Cox, there are five "domains of experience that activate strong threats and rewards in the brain, thus influencing a wide range of human behaviors."[4] These domains are status, certainty, autonomy, relatedness, and fairness. The NeuroLeadership Institute combines them into a handy acronym: SCARF. These are essential human needs—as important, if not more important than what we normally think of as basic human needs like food and shelter. After all, humans are social creatures. We are most successful at feeding ourselves, finding shelter, and staying physically safe when we relate to and collaborate with other humans. Without that, chances of surviving, let alone thriving, are not great.

3. https://rework.withgoogle.com/print/guides/5721312655835136/
4. Dr. David Rock and Christine Cox, Ph.D., "SCARF ® in 2012: Updating the Social Neuroscience of Collaborating with Others," *NeuroLeadership Journal*, 2012.

S TATUS
C ERTAINTY
A UTONOMY
R ELATEDNESS
F AIRNESS

BASED ON DAVE GRAY'S VERSION, WITH PERMISSION, AS SEEN IN *LIMINAL THINKING*

You perform at your best when you are certain of what's to come, have agency over your actions, are connected to those around you, and feel that you're treated fairly. This is the case in life and especially in the workplace. In the absence of these rewards, you feel the opposite—under threat.

Even though Akshay was the boss, he was having a few key psychological safety buttons pushed—status, certainty, and relatedness. He was Lilia's manager, yet he was convinced that his status was undermined when he prescribed solutions that she did not follow. He could not count on things getting done or goals being met, which led to a lot of uncertainty. And he was frustrated and disappointed as a result. The more frustrated he got, the more he dictated solutions, and the more frustrated Lilia got, the more their relationship suffered.

On the flip side, many of Lilia's psychological safety buttons were being pushed as well. After all, her boss was constantly frustrated, avoiding her, or telling her what to do. One day, she'd be afraid of losing her job, and the next she'd be ready to quit. This not only impacted their relationship, but it impacted her performance…which also made things worse. They argued or they avoided one another. In between the situation and his reactions, Akshay wrote Lilia's story for her, which made him react even worse when under stress. He was convinced that she was a liability rather than an asset. This story wrote their collective story with a terrible ending: he needed to fire her.

As we dug a little deeper, pulling out all the stories Akshay was telling himself about Lilia and the situation they were in and how he felt about it, he suddenly looked like he was ready to cry. Beneath the frustration and disappointment, he was sad.

"I don't think she likes me," he said, earnestly after a long pause. "I'm afraid that she doesn't care about what we're building."

"You look sad. What's going on?"

"Yeah, I'm sad. And honestly, I'm terrified."

At this point, we had a better handle on the situation.

The facts were that Lilia was new, a mom, a COO, and not meeting her goals.

Akshay felt frustrated, disappointed, and dejected. He was also afraid. He had just raised a lot of money, and he had a lot riding on the success of his company. All true.

The stories that Akshay had created in his mind were that Lilia was not cut out to do this job. She didn't like Akshay, and she wasn't engaged in their mission. He had a horror story lurking in the shadows: if things continued this way, the company would fail. And he had a problematically insidious story woven throughout—the kind of yarn that is unfortunately spun when gender, politics, race, sexuality, or ethnicity are at play: a mom who spent time with her kids could not be an effective executive.

While facts and feelings are true, the fiction that you tell yourself when you're facing difficult situations *feels* true. But it's a fantasy until you prove otherwise. In other words, it might be true. Or not. You've got to find out.

For example, was the story about the company failing if Lilia didn't meet their shared goals true or false? Technically, that could eventually happen. But the rest? There was only one way to find out.

Akshay had to have a brave conversation.

"Have you heard of the SBI Feedback Model?" I asked.

"Maybe?" he responded. Like most leaders I work with who have a corporate background, Akshay had sat through countless management trainings over the years—but he rarely remembered what he had learned, nor did he figure out how to apply it effectively.

"I don't know. Maybe not. Tell me."

The 3Fs Model

It's the rare person who likes having to give positive or negative feedback, confront people in tough situations, or have difficult conversations. The thing is, when you're a leader, you *have* to do these things—it's your job.

There are countless feedback and difficult conversation frameworks and models out there: SBI (Situation, Behavior, Impact),[5] COIN (Context, Observation, Impact, Next Steps),[6] Nonviolent Communication (NVC),[7] Crucial Conversations,[8] and Radical Candor,[9] to name a few. They're all excellent. But the folks I work with find them difficult to remember and even harder to apply in real time and in real-life situations.

---

5. www.ccl.org/articles/leading-effectively-articles/closing-the-gap-between-intent-vs-impact-sbii/
6. Anna Carroll, *The Feedback Imperative: How to Give Everyday Feedback to Speed Up Your Team's Success* (Austin, TX: River Grove Books, 2014).
7. Marshall B. Rosenberg, Ph.D., *Nonviolent Communication: A Language of Life: Life-Changing Tools for Healthy Relationships*, 3rd ed. (Encinitas, CA: PuddleDancer Press, 2015).
8. Kerry Patterson, Joseph Grenny, Ron McMillan, and Al Switzler, *Crucial Conversations: Tools for Talking When Stakes Are High*, 3rd ed. (New York: McGraw Hill, 2021).
9. Kim Scott, *Radical Candor: Be a Kick-Ass Boss Without Losing Your Humanity*, fully revised and updated ed. (New York: St. Martin's Press, 2019).

One thing these frameworks all have in common is that they all involve big stories: something happened that impacted your ability to meet your needs or goals. When you present that to the other person and ask them to take some kind of action, you're writing a better ending to your story.

These frameworks account for little stories—insidious fictions—that might be making the issue worse rather than better. "When you submitted the report with many errors last week, it delayed us by three days. We need to be working faster. How can we prevent that in the future?" is a lot more actionable than "Why are you always so careless?! Be more careful!" The former is true, while the latter is probably not.

The reason you focus on behavior and observations when giving feedback is that it's important for people to know exactly what is wrong and what the impact is rather than your probably wrong interpretation. For example, I can't tell you how many times my clients have been frustrated by someone's "carelessness" when the issue was rooted in understaffing, broken workflows, or someone not exercising their superpowers on projects. It's important and most effective to check your fictions before you take the wrong actions. You'll save lots of time, energy, and frustration.

When you see the stories in what you collectively want to accomplish and what's getting in your way, you can check and rewrite your stories—alone and with others—so that your stories ultimately get you to where you want to go. To do that, however, you need not only situations, behaviors, and impact. You also need feelings. After all, it's not just words or stories that move people to action. It's the feelings that they have that ultimately alert, inspire, and motivate them.

Feelings will help you connect with your side of the story as well as connect with the other person. In the end, "When you submitted the report with many errors last week, it delayed us by three days. I'm disappointed and frustrated since this has been happening a lot lately. But I'm also confused because I thought you were excited to work on this project. What's going on?" will get you to where you want to go. It's heartfelt, it's honest, and most importantly, it's all true. It's an invitation to receive the same in return.

While effective feedback usually involves facts and feelings, and checking your fictions before you talk to someone, there are times when you can play with this. When you cultivate a culture of psychological safety and have strong relationships with those you work with, then this conversation might get you to the bottom of the story quickly and effectively: "Here's a story I'm telling myself that may or may not be true: I'm worried that you hate working on these reports. They're full of so many errors!" As long as you understand that you're presenting your side of the story and invite the other person to collaborate on a better ending, you'll get to where you want to go.

Facts, Feelings, and Fiction

Next time you're facing challenging situations with other people remember the 3Fs—facts, feelings, and fiction.

First, you have to separate your *facts*, *feelings*, and *fiction*. Something happened, and you told yourself a story that may or may not be true about the situation, more likely about the other person. You had feelings. Feelings compelled you to take action. But often it's the wrong action. That's *your* part of the story—you need to pull apart what's really happening.

Next, you need to stop, pause, and admire your natural ability to see stories everywhere. Remember, if you're making up stories, your brain is just doing its job to protect you. Appreciate your ability to show up and keep yourself safe. When you can fully and wholeheartedly appreciate something—even your outsized or otherwise misguided reactions to situations—your nervous system will calm down. Your pulse slows, your vision widens, and your brain is better able to solve problems. This is important. You're going to need that problem-solving ability to move on to the next step.

Then you need to understand the other person's story—facts, feelings, and potentially any fiction—so that you can co-create a better ending and meet your basic human needs and shared, key goals.

If you use any of the previous models, this is a layer you can add to make them more effective. And if you don't, you can use this on its own. I'd pull facts, feelings, fiction, understanding, co-creating, and key goals into a handy, cheeky acronym for you. But then this book would be no longer safe for work—which is not ideal for a business book. Just remember that while resolving conflict can feel hard and scary, it doesn't have to be. At its best, it's a creative, collaborative exercise in storytelling—a key part in the leader's journey.

A Better Ending

When Akshay eventually met with Lilia, he laid it all out there. He started by reminding her why he started the company, why he hired her, why he admired her, and what he wanted them to accomplish together. He then reiterated their more tactical goals—the ones that weren't being met and how concerned he was about that. Facts and feelings. He then earnestly presented the fiction that was driving his concerns.

"This may or may not be true." Akshay said. "But I'm afraid that you're just not so into the company and that's why you're not meeting your goals and deadlines. I'm also worried that if things keep going this way, we'll be out of business in a few years. Worst of all," he continued, "I'm worried that you don't think I'm a good CEO. Whenever I make suggestions, you shrug them off. I'm not really sure what to do anymore." It was a lot. But it was all finally out there.

After Akshay presented his side of things, he paused. He took a deep breath. And he simply asked, "What's up?"

Inviting someone to tell you their side of the story is often that simple and straightforward. In Akshay's case, he was the boss, so it was fine for him to present his half of the story and invite Lilia in with a simple

"What's up?" He was coming to her from a place of privilege and a sincere desire to know what was going on.

When the power dynamic is flipped or your issue is with someone you don't manage, you can still present your side. But you'll want to choose your words accordingly. What matters most is not exactly what you say, but how you say it. To resolve conflict effectively, you have to be open, honest, and ultimately genuinely curious—about the other person and about how you might resolve things together.

On the one hand, Lilia was surprised to hear all this from Akshay. On the other hand, she was glad that he was finally bringing it up. She was as frustrated as he was with how things were going. She was afraid that she had accepted the wrong job. And she was also afraid of losing her job.

Despite Lilia's brash, confident façade, she was operating from a place of fear as much as Akshay was. She was a woman working in a workplace dominated by men; she was a mom in a workplace dominated by younger, child-free engineers; and she was new to the company. By default, her status, certainty, and relatedness were things she either had to earn or fight to receive. She tried not to think about it most of the time and was generally preoccupied with more typical new-job workplace jitters. But it was in the back of her mind as she spun her experiences with Akshay into unflattering narratives and reacted in kind.

In this moment, however, she was calm and intrigued by his openness and curiosity. She trusted him enough to answer frankly.

"Akshay," she said. "I've been here for three months. I'm still learning. I'm still ramping up my team. And I'm still getting a feel for the culture. It takes time to onboard at a new company and to step into a role like this. I'm trying my best."

Lilia had set some aggressive goals with Akshay when she started, hoping that she would meet them by the end of the quarter. It was true—she had not met them. But there was someone in her way: Akshay.

"Akshay," she continued, "you're a very involved CEO, and I appreciate that. However, you come to us every week, and you tell us what to do. One week, we're focusing on innovation, the next we're building out a sales organization for a product that we don't even have. My team is frustrated. I'm frustrated. They're constantly coming to me saying, 'Get Akshay out of our meetings. He's a micromanager. He's a control freak!' I worry that they're right, but I tell them you're involved in all the details because you care. At least I assume that's why you do what you do. You have so many ideas of how things should be. My team wants to please you. I want to please you. But ultimately, Akshay, you're slowing us down. I love you. But please let me do my job. I'm new. I just started. I know I can do this."

That was Lilia's side of the story. It was a lot. But it was all there. Facts, feelings, and fiction. Akshay couldn't argue with any of it. And he didn't need to clarify any of it. Because it was all true.

For the first time in a long time, Akshay understood Lilia's side of the story. He had worked for micromanagers before. It was extremely frustrating, and it was one of the reasons why he started his own company—so he wouldn't have to follow someone else's orders and changing whims. Yet here he was doing to other people exactly what he spent his career trying to avoid.

"I'm not giving you much autonomy, am I?" he asked as he recalled what I taught him about basic human needs. "I wouldn't perform well in that case, either."

It turns out that not having autonomy to do her job was Lilia's kryptonite. Out of all of the basic human needs, it was the one she valued more than the others. Not having it infuriated her. But Akshay was the boss. Without the status or certainty that she needed to call him out on it, she instead reacted by trying to avoid him as much as possible or snapped at him when they were in meetings. She didn't realize that she was doing it. She was embarrassed by her reactions. But she was too caught up in it all to fix the situation. Plus, it wasn't her job. Her job was to run operations for the company, not take care of her CEO.

As Lilia and Akshay talked, they started to see each other as real people again. They were no longer faceless drivers cutting each other off on a busy highway. They were two people who respected each other, appreciated each other, and had signed on for what they hoped would be a long and fruitful partnership revolutionizing how people received healthcare.

"I wonder what we should do about this?" Akshay asked, inviting Lilia to collaborate on a better ending to their story. "Because as much as I understand where you're coming from, I need to feel more confident that we'll meet our numbers. I really want to trust you, but I need more than blind faith."

In the end, Akshay and Lilia recommitted to having their weekly one-on-ones, something they had stopped doing because they got so painful. And they agreed to keep checking in with each other's facts, feelings, and fiction whenever they needed to in between. Akshay agreed to give Lilia another quarter to move the needle. And Lilia agreed to be forthright with Akshay if she had any serious concerns about the viability of the business or her ability to help him grow the company.

And then he asked, "What do you need from me?" which was critically important to the success of this co-created story.

"I need you to trust me," replied Lilia.

Akshay wondered if he could trust her. His gut said yes, but his heart was afraid. Regardless, he found himself saying, "I'll try." He cracked a smile, and they both laughed. It was the first time in a while that they not only saw each other as people, but shared something that wasn't avoidance, ill-feelings, and terse words.

Rather than wait another three months, they decided to try things out for a week and see how it went. That way, they could renegotiate or reorient if necessary. Akshay was excited to see what would happen next.

They went with their plan for the next quarter, and now they got along great. They've since figured out how to work together—how to be open, honest, forthcoming, and transparent with each other. And they have difficult conversations when they need to.

Akshay even started sharing positive feedback with Lilia more routinely to make sure they both understood what was working and how to make that happen more often. Positive feedback is its own kind of difficult conversation because many of us feel as uncomfortable giving it as we do receiving it. But when you present facts and feelings—what you see and how you feel, the true story—and you invite the other person to share their facts and feelings, that's a good story. It's one that you can't argue with. And it's one that works much better than blanket praise.

In the end, Akshay learned how to trust his COO. Lilia learned how to trust her CEO. It wasn't always easy, but they made it work. This didn't just make things better for him and her, but also for her team and the entire company. That's a much better story than what was and could have been.

10

Reflecting On Your Journey

W hen Kai first brought up the topic of business going well, she was perplexed. Her company was scaling quickly and things were going well. But after years of nonstop hustling, her team was cranky and uncooperative. Metrics were good, but morale was low. She knew from previous experience that if this continued, metrics would eventually suffer. She wanted to fix this before it became a problem.

She tried adding company benefits and perks to increase morale—performance bonuses, tickets to baseball games, free lunches on Tuesdays. People appreciated the sentiment and the perks, but the situation did not improve. Kai was burned out. Her team was burned out. People across her company were burned out.

As such, Kai didn't feel much like a hero and neither did anyone else in the organization. It turns out that she needed to do less, not more. Only then would she enable those she worked with to rebuild their energy to eventually do more.

The Art of Closure

Imagine your latest Netflix binge. With no episodes. Just a loooooong moving picture that lasts hours and hours. Four? Nine? Thirteen hours?

An adventure that never ends.

Your brain would not be happy.

There's a reason for this: Your brain needs closure to learn, rest, and then build energy for what's next. It's why movies have scenes, books have chapters, and TV shows have episodes.

Burnout happens when things are not going well, and especially when things are going *really* well and you want to keep going. You burn out when you don't complete cycles of experience.

At key points along your journey, whether it's a set period of time, a milestone, or some success along the way, you need to stop and take stock of all you and those around you have accomplished.

If you don't take time to reflect on and make meaning of your experience with more than a "good job!" or financial bonus, your story might as well have never happened. And if it didn't happen, you will find it difficult to calm down, feel good, and build energy and ideas for how to level up and amplify your success next time. This is what was happening to Kai and her team.

Looking back at the end of a journey and gleaning meaning from what you've accomplished is very, very important for closing one story and moving on to the next one in your life. Whether you are reflecting on your own journey as an individual, team, or organization, or inviting someone else to reflect on theirs, the best way to do that is—you guessed it—a story.

To recap your story, ask five simple questions:

- What did I/we/you want to accomplish?
- What did I/we/you accomplish?
- What did I/we/you learn?
- What impact did I/we/you make?
- How will I/we/you celebrate?

That last question is particularly important. Celebrating is the happy ending to the best stories, and it's also a productive ending to a year, quarter, or project. Celebrating is not only fun, but it's also important for a couple of reasons. First, celebrating gives you real, actual closure rather than a sort-of closure. It engages your physical and emotional being, which is something that you often miss when you engage in intellectual pursuits.

When you move onto the next shiny thing without getting complete closure on an experience, your brain never gets the chance to settle down, relax, and recharge so that it can better rev up for the next exciting episode or difficult challenge. So what seems trivial is actually important.

Celebrate. Once you take time to reflect and at least plan your celebration, you'll start building energy for what's next, which is important. You'll need that energy to make your next episode, next season, and next level even better than the last.

Building Your Reflective Practice

When Kai and I first discussed the idea of building her reflective practice—personally, with her team, and across her company—she was reluctant. Like most of the companies I work with, Kai's company had robust goalsetting and reporting systems. That's how they knew they were doing so well.

Every quarter, each executive created a report to summarize what objectives they met and metrics that had changed. Then the executive team would collaborate on new goals for the next quarter in preparation for their next board meeting. They typically did this by sharing documents or sometimes by meeting at an off-site retreat.

Some teams also did retrospectives and postmortems—reviews of what went well, and what did not—at the end of sprints, projects, or quarters. Those were often done in long meetings where people checked off lists or moved tasks around on boards and mostly complained about what went wrong. People dreaded those meetings. So much so that they often skipped them entirely. And all teams did annual 360-degree performance reviews. People dreaded those just as much, if not more, because the feedback was personal.

Kai's team and company had systems. But they were missing the story.

"What should we do?" Kai asked. She was desperate to change things and open to ideas.

"What do you have in mind?"

"I knew you'd ask that. Just tell me!" she said with the glee of someone who had a million ideas ready to go but didn't want to share them because she assumed they were terrible. Sometimes she just wanted me to tell her what to do so that she could argue with me. It is a fun sport that a lot of my clients like to engage in. As much as I would have liked to share a surefire way to build reflective practice into how she worked, it was a stance rather than a process. It was something she would need to play with and develop over time.

"Would you like a reflection worksheet to try?" I asked. "You can use it yourself or share it with your team."

"Yes, please."

"I have only one condition. Make it your own."

"What do you mean?"

"You can ask everyone to start filling out a reflection survey, for example. Or force people to use the framework in meetings or transform how you do 360s. But nobody wants you to give them more work to do," I said. "If you add yet another tool, approach, or framework to how you work, you're going to meet resistance. It's what's been happening so far, and this is no different. But if you can figure out a way to make this approach and thinking a part of how you work and how everyone else works, you will find much more success using it."

I gave Kai a few examples of how other clients have integrated reflective practice into their work, and she was intrigued. Some of my clients like to bake story-driven questions into their existing retrospectives, meetings, or performance reviews. Others have never had a practice of doing retrospectives in the first place, and they use it as a framework to build from. And the most successful ones started looking for stories *everywhere*—in one-on-one meetings with direct reports, official meetings, coffees, presentations, reports, and more. They learned over time how to see what was working and reflect that to other people, thereby helping them all feel better and work better.

When you develop a habit of reflecting on your stories—big and small—it becomes a part of how you work and ultimately how you think. The more that happens, the more you will start to see these stories everywhere. Not only will you be able to reflect on them yourself, but you'll also be able to reflect them to other people.

When you do this in the moment, psychologists call this *active constructive responding.*[1] You can do this informally, for example, when someone comes to you to share a success, or when you have a small win. Studies show that the more you do this, the more confident, happy, connected, and committed you will feel. Or you can do it more formally—alone or with a group of people—at a project milestone or at the end of a quarter, project, or year. This is what Kai and her team eventually figured out.

Kai didn't want to upend any of their processes or add more work to people's workload, so she started her reflective practice by looking for stories that people told her in one-on-one conversations. What she found surprised her.

Her one-on-one meetings used to feel like progress reports. They were painful, and she often skipped them as a result. But once she started seeing the story in what her executives told her—or asked questions that got the story out of people—and reflected that back to them, the

---

1. Kate Hood, "The Benefits of Active Constructive Responding," Geelong Grammar School, October 13, 2021.

energy started to shift. People often weren't aware of what they had accomplished—big things and especially the small wins—and neither was Kai. They were surprised to find out that she was paying attention.

By asking people a handful of questions to pull their stories out of them, she helped them feel like heroes. The same thing happened when she did it for herself. It was a simple practice that made a noticeable difference.

Over time, people started coming to her with *their* wins without her even asking. It felt good. That wasn't a feeling that she or the others in the organization had had in quite a while.

Eventually, once she started to see a shift in how she ran her meetings with individuals, Kai started to bake some of this practice into her executive team meetings. It shifted the conversation for the better. This was helpful because, by the time she brought up the idea of modifying the way they ran retrospectives and goal-setting meetings with her head of engineering and chief people officer, they were receptive rather than resistant.

They had noticed how their executive team meetings had changed over the previous few months. They had noticed the slight shift in perspective that Kai had when she talked with people. And they *felt* the difference—they felt more appreciated, heard, and accomplished.

In the weeks and months that followed, they started figuring out their own ways of seeing stories in the work that they did, alone and with their teams. What had felt like a chore became a core part of how they worked. So much so that they didn't even realize when they were doing it most of the time.

It's not surprising. That's when stories are most effective—when they are invisible. But Kai didn't just see this shift reflected in how she and others felt. It also showed in their performance surveys, and the fact that people not only came to the next company party but they actually had fun at it. A detail like that might seem insignificant compared to business metrics and returns, but it was important to Kai. She knew from past experience that the better she and everyone else felt, the better they would sustain their performance over the long run.

But that was beside the point. She didn't just build her company to make money or even just to have fun for fun's sake—she wanted to make a positive impact on people's lives. And by transforming everyone into heroes who owned their stories, she was able to do just that.

11

Own Your Story

In the 2021 film, *Spider-Man: No Way Home*, Peter Parker has a problem. After causing significant damage while saving the day, the press paints Spider-Man (and his newly outed alter-ego Peter Parker) as a public menace. As a result, Peter loses friends and struggles to achieve his and Spider-Man's goals: go to college while also saving the world. He spends a lot of time trying to tell anyone who will listen that he's not a villain—he's a superhero! But the more he yells, the less people listen.

For the public to understand who Peter really is and the impact that he can really have, he needs to stop telling and do more doing. When he does, people finally see him for what he is: a superhero who saves the day. Once they see and experience that, they tell his story for him. As a result, he amplifies his impact because people work with him rather than against him.

Leadership works much the same way. When Lane, the VP of Engineering at a fintech startup, was promoted to her first executive role, she had a similar challenge. She had worked her way up to the top ranks of her company and knew that she was the right person for the job. But when her first round of performance reviews came along, she was shocked and dismayed. The biggest complaint? "Stop it with the storytelling."

When Lane first came to see me for help, she didn't understand why she had received that particular bit of feedback. She had worked for years to sharpen her storytelling chops. People said that tech leaders need to be great storytellers to balance how technical they were. She did that! And now her colleagues were complaining about it.

When Lane told stories, the people she worked with struggled to connect with her and her accomplishments on a personal level. She was great at talking—explaining, telling, and demonstrating technical concepts—but she didn't do a lot of listening. And she often forgot to demonstrate enough of what her company wanted from her: leadership capabilities.

As a result, people felt like she was talking *at* them instead of working with them. This didn't leave a lot of room for her team to feel very super. And when they didn't feel super, they did not perform well. Similar to Peter Parker, the more Lane talked about being a leader, the less she acted like a leader.

What both Peter Parker and Lane eventually learned (and what I hope you have learned through reading this book) is that the stories you tell are only as effective as the stories you bring to life. The most powerful stories are the ones you demonstrate—through your beliefs, actions, and interactions with other people. Telling stories is important. But it's only a tiny part of how you make an impact as a leader. In fact, if you do it too much, you may very well decrease your impact.

Your story as a leader starts with an inner core of understanding who you are and where you're going. If it starts with telling, it is a flimsy eggshell that is waiting to crack under pressure.

This is what I wished I had known on that fateful day with that executive team in Napa many years ago. It's what I now help the super leaders I have the honor of working with realize. And it's what I am sharing with you. Your stories flow through you and everything you do. They are your hopes, your dreams, your fears, your relationships, your journeys, your thoughts, your actions, and your emotions. Your stories are the impact you make in the world. And your stories are the most powerful when you co-create them and invite the world to own and experience them with you.

You *are* your stories.

The most powerful story is you.

Your leadership is comprised of what you tell yourself, what you tell other people, the journeys you go on, the obstacles you face, and the difference you make in the world. The more you feel like a hero, the more you can empower others to be heroes of their own stories and your collective stories, and you can achieve the extraordinary. Because as a leader, you and your stories are amplified by the stories you help others experience.

Once you see stories in everything that you do, you too can be a hero. In transforming yourself into more of who you really are, you will transform your world.

What's your story?

What do you want your story to be?

How will you bring your best story to life?

Index

 **Rosenfeld®**

Dear Reader,

Thanks very much for purchasing this book. There's a story behind it and every product we create at Rosenfeld Media.

Since the early 1990s, I've been a User Experience consultant, conference presenter, workshop instructor, and author. (I'm probably best-known for having cowritten *Information Architecture for the Web and Beyond*.) In each of these roles, I've been frustrated by the missed opportunities to apply UX principles and practices.

I started Rosenfeld Media in 2005 with the goal of publishing books whose design and development showed that a publisher could practice what it preached. Since then, we've expanded into producing industry-leading conferences and workshops. In all cases, UX has helped us create better, more successful products—just as you would expect. From employing user research to drive the design of our books and conference programs, to working closely with our conference speakers on their talks, to caring deeply about customer service, we practice what we preach every day.

Please visit **rosenfeldmedia.com** to learn more about our **conferences**, **workshops**, **free communities**, and **other great resources** that we've made for you. And send your ideas, suggestions, and concerns my way: louis@rosenfeldmedia.com

I'd love to hear from you, and I hope you enjoy the book!

Lou Rosenfeld

Lou Rosenfeld,
Publisher

RECENT TITLES FROM ROSENFELD MEDIA

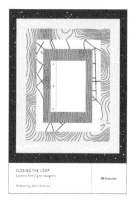 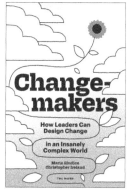 

Get a great discount on a Rosenfeld Media book:
visit rfld.me/deal to learn more.

SELECTED TITLES FROM ROSENFELD MEDIA

  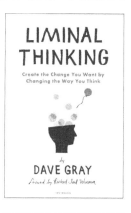

 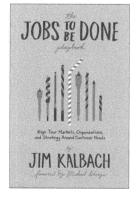 

View our full catalog at rosenfeldmedia.com/books

Acknowledgments

To my partner, Erica, who somehow thought it was doable for us to undertake a home renovation, book, jobs, and parent two littles at the same time. Whoops. We did it!

To my kids, Max and Micah, and nieces, Shina and Mirina, who constantly remind me of what having confidence and a cape can look like. To my clients who do the same—I am in awe of what you can and will continue to achieve.

To Peter Economy who helped me get this book out of my head. And Lou Rosenfeld, Marta Justak, and MJ Broadbent, who helped me get it onto paper.

To Christina Wodtke, Andrea Mignolo, and Irene Salter who helped me make this book make sense—and especially to Christina for being on speed dial throughout my writer's journey and beyond. To Lis Hubert, Jane Pirone, Madonnalisa Chan, Christina Berkley, Roz Duffy, Margot Bloomstein, Tutti Taygerly, Kate McKean, Josh Seiden, Petra Wille, Jeff Gothelf, Scott Berkun, Hatchlings, Art of Action, Boss Ladies, Eggheads, and many others I know I'm forgetting for advising and cheerleading me along the way.

And to the amazing faculty at the Gestalt International Study Center in Cape Cod, who taught me how to stop trying to change things and instead appreciate what is. I've created more lasting change—for myself, my family, and the world—this way than ever before.

About the Author

DONNA LICHAW is an executive coach, keynote speaker, and author of the bestselling book, *The User's Journey: Storymapping Products That People Love.* Her mission is to help unconventional leaders transform their impact so that they can effect positive change in the world.

Donna works with superheroes and teams of superheroes at companies like Google, Disney, Twitter, Microsoft, Mailchimp, and Adobe, as well as a plethora of startups and nonprofits.

She has been on the adjunct faculty at New York University, Northwestern University, Parsons School of Design, and the School of Visual Arts. When she's not working, you can find her hanging out in Brooklyn, NY, with her partner, Erica, superkids, Max and Micah, and superdog, Ralph.

Find out how to work with Donna as well as access her free newsletter, toolkit, exercises, workshops, courses, and more at donnalichaw.com.

CPSIA information can be obtained
at www.ICGtesting.com
Printed in the USA
JSHW012245060423
39887JS00003B/5

9 781959 029137